Economic Myths and Magic

Economic Myths and Magic

Debunking the Illusions of Conventional
Economic Thinking

Norman C. Miller

*Professor of Economics, Farmer School of Business, Miami
University, USA*

Edward Elgar
PUBLISHING

Cheltenham, UK • Northampton, MA, USA

Published by
Edward Elgar Publishing Limited
The Lypiatts
15 Lansdown Road
Cheltenham
Glos GL50 2JA
UK

Edward Elgar Publishing, Inc.
William Pratt House
9 Dewey Court
Northampton
Massachusetts 01060
USA

Paperback edition 2024

A catalogue record for this book
is available from the British Library

Library of Congress Control Number: 2023931306

This book is available electronically in the **Elgar**online
Economics subject collection
http://dx.doi.org/10.4337/9781803925639

ISBN 978 1 80392 562 2 (cased)
ISBN 978 1 80392 563 9 (eBook)
ISBN 978 1 0353 3903 7 (paperback)

Printed and bound by CPI Group (UK) Ltd, Croydon, CR0 4YY

Contents

Figures

Tables

Preface

It is high time that someone debunks many of the myths about our economy. That is the main objective here. Some of these myths are: (a) imports always reduce GDP and domestic jobs; (b) trickle-down theory is no longer operative; (c) taxing the rich to help the poor and achieve a more equal distribution of income reduces incentives and decreases economic growth rates; (d) US balance of trade deficits have generated a net loss of millions of jobs; (e) immigrants reduce jobs for Americans and cause more unemployment; (f) a higher minimum wage leads to an overall loss of jobs and increases unemployment; (g) computers and robots will eventually eliminate a huge percentage of all jobs, and generate excessive unemployment; and (h) since a country cannot persistently produce more than its potential output (Yp) any aggregate demand that exceeds Yp will ultimately have no effect on output or jobs; it simply increases prices.

Every one of the myths seems reasonable, but none of them are true, and many might be absolutely the reverse of the truth. Why? First, many myths represent a naïve extrapolation of a tautological statement such as: (a) if a robot does a job, then of course a human does not do it; and (b) if a product is imported, then of course it was not produced in the receiving country. People have unwittingly jumped from such statements to unproven assertions about the entire economy.

Second, some of the myths come from sound *microeconomic* principles, e.g., 'if wage rates are higher, then firms will tend to hire less labor.' This is true, but from a *macroeconomic* perspective higher wage rates increase aggregate demand, and this creates jobs. Equivalently, excessive imports cause firms to downsize and/or go out of business, thereby reducing employment. Again, this is true, but excessive imports indirectly can help an economy grow faster, thereby generating many new jobs.

Third, we have not completely figured out how a complex economy functions. If we had, then there would not be so many different schools of thought that often yield conflicting statements and/or advice about the economy. If people do not understand how the real world works then it is relatively easy for them to accept a myth.

The book makes it abundantly clear that there is much that we do not know. When everything in the economy has turned out better than our current theories predict, this is attributed figuratively to 'economic magic'. When everything has fallen apart for the economy (e.g., the Great Depression, the Great Recession, and the COVID-19 pandemic) we blame 'economic black magic'. More realistically, 'magic' and 'black magic' refer to phenomena that are not formally incorporated into conventional macroeconomic thinking, such as the effects of optimism or pessimism; fear and panic; too much or not enough regulation; insufficient competition; biased economic data; and 'bad' economic theories (ignorance).

To a large extent economists talk to each other via conferences, scholarly books, and scholarly journal articles. It often takes years before an important new idea finds its way into a textbook and/or into mainstream thinking. The general public needs to be kept up to date, especially with regard to recent critiques of economic thinking. I know of no important economic theory that cannot be explained clearly to educated people. Anyone who ever reads *Business Week*, *The Economist*, the *Wall Street Journal*, etc. will be able to understand this book.

Much of what appears here is known to professional economists with particular specialties. Hopefully, those with such specialties will obtain a new perspective on topics in which they have not specialized. I trust that professional economists will tolerate my brief reviews of what they already know. Finally, the reader is warned that a few of the ideas here will be considered 'absolute heresy'. However, someone needs to step up and say 'but the Emperor has no clothes'.

In my career I have been fortunate to have associated with many outstanding economists that include: Marina Whitman, Daniel McFadden, Peter Kenen, Dick Roll, Bob Lucas, Mort Kamien, Nancy Schwartz, Al Roth, and Wassily Leontief. Many of them contributed to my education during and beyond graduate school. All of them showed me what it means to pursue excellence, and encouraged me to do so. In addition, I would like to thank those who provided useful comments on the manuscript, especially Reilly Cirenza, Xufeng He, Doug Miller, and Nathan Miller.

Abbreviations

ARM	Adjustable Rate Mortgage
ATM	Automatic Teller Machine
CBO	Congressional Budget Office
CBOE	Chicago Board Options Exchange
CPI	Consumer Price Index
DJIA	Dow Jones Industrial Average
E[MRPL]	expected value of the marginal revenue product of labor
FDI	foreign direct investment
FDIC	Federal Deposit Insurance Corporation
FFR	Federal Funds Rate
FPI	foreign portfolio investment
FRED	Federal Reserve Economic Data
FX	foreign exchange
ICC	Interstate Commerce Commission
IPOs	initial public offerings
LFPR	labor force participation rate
M1	(coins and currency in circulation) + (all checkable accounts) + (savings accounts) + (travelers' checks)
M2	M1 + MMFs + small time deposits
MMF	money market fund
MRPL	marginal revenue product of labor
NRH	Natural Rate Hypothesis
PCE	Personal Consumption Expenditure
RGPDI	Real Gross Private Direct Investment
WTO	World Trade Organization

1. Myths and magic: introduction, objectives, and preview

1.1   INTRODUCTION

I am disturbed about the many half-truths, deceptive and/or false statements uttered by politicians, the media, and even some economists. We hear one story about the economy from conservative politicians, newspapers, and cable TV news programs and a completely different story from the liberal side of things. Furthermore, poor forecasts (especially of inflation) as well as the fact that economists always seem to disagree have reduced the profession's credibility. Something needs to be done. Thomas Philippon believes that economists should be able to challenge the conventional wisdom, and take a contrarian perspective.[1] This book does exactly that!

We rarely hear someone say that they simply do not know. Let me say right up front that I do not have it all figured out ... and probably no one does. The economy is infinitely complex. Every dot in the picture on this book's cover is connected to every other dot, often in many round-about ways. The economy is much more complex than this.

Many myths about the workings of the entire economy, i.e., macroeconomics, are simply theoretical extrapolations of microeconomic theories, or, worse yet, of tautological statements. Furthermore, traditionally microeconomic theory does not take account of real-world complexities such as fear, optimism versus pessimism, greed, corruption, too much or too little government regulation, etc.[2] Also, scholars have only relatively recently explored how income inequality (or the perception of it) can affect economic behavior. *The economic myths exist, in part, because we have not yet figured out the infinite complexity of a modern economy.* Figuratively speaking, the myths exist because of economic magic and economic black magic.

The position taken in this book is that we simply do not know the answers to many important questions such as: (a) does a higher minimum wage reduce employment or increase it by creating jobs throughout the economy?; (b) do international trade and advances in technology decrease the standards of living for a significant number of people, or do they simply make them feel left behind because they have not gained as much as others?; (c) do international trade deficits decrease jobs or, alternatively, increase jobs by stimulating economic growth?; and (d) does greater income inequality create strong incentives that ultimately stimulate economic growth?

Economic magic is figuratively given credit in this book for those time intervals when everything seemed to work out miraculously well. For example, why did the US unemployment rate for men not rise persistently when more than 10 million women entered the labor force from 1949 until 1969? Why have millions of immigrant workers from Mexico not increased overall unemployment in the USA? Why was the US unemployment rate at a 49-year low at the end of 2019 when the USA had been consistently experiencing annual balance of trade deficits of $400 billion to $500 billion? Alternatively, we blame black magic on those intervals when everything seemed to fall apart. Three examples are: the Great Depression, the Great Recession, and the COVID-19 pandemic.

1.2   OBJECTIVES

The main objective here is to debunk many commonly held illusions about the economy. This endeavor lays bare many things that we do not know ... and this is a surprisingly large set. The book contains many ideas that are known by economists with narrow specialties but are not known in general. More importantly, much of what is known by scholars has not filtered down to conventional thinking in textbooks, the media, the political arena., and the educated population. The reader is warned, however, that some of what appears here will be labeled as *absolute heresy*, e.g., a higher minimum wage or trade balance deficits can conceivably increase employment. But someone has to have the courage to say that 'the emperor has no clothes!'

Behavioral Economics has taken account of some of the complexities of human behavior that have not been included in traditional microeconomic thinking. This activity has spilled over into Behavioral Macroeconomics that focuses on the behavior of households, businesses, and investors which affect the entire economy, but are not a part of traditional macroeconomic thinking.[3]

A second objective here is to address how the overall economy is affected by: (a) pessimism, fear and panic versus optimism; (b) competition (especially foreign competition) or the lack of it; (c) too much or too little government regulation; (d) bad or just plain wrong macroeconomic theories, i.e., ignorance; (e) false or misleading data; and (f) economic hysteresis.[4]

A third objective is to use the concepts (as defined here) of economic magic and black magic to explain: (a) why the US economy performed well over most of the three or four decades before the COVID-19 pandemic. This success occurred in spite of obvious shortcomings in the economy, and several extremely negative shocks; and (b) why the economy fell apart in the 1930s, in 2007–2008, and in 2020.

COVID-19 wreaked havoc on the world economy, but it became abundantly clear that we are all in it together! This applies to much more than the USA versus the rest of the world. It also applies to every aspect of the US economy. All industries, firms, families, and workers are inexorably tied together in an infinitely complex manner. A fourth objective here is to offer a new perspective on this complexity.

It is well known that any positive or negative spending shock to an economy can be transmitted throughout the economy via the 'multiplier' effect. For example, an exogenous increase in government spending will initially increase the incomes of many firms and workers. These workers and firms will then spend more, thereby raising the incomes of more people, who, in turn, spend more, etc., etc., etc. The multiplier transmission mechanism is *downstream* in nature. It exists because of Say's Law and Keynes' Law, as defined in Chapter 3.

The new perspective here is *upstream* in nature. We know via any Leontief type of input/output table that a significant change in the output of any one good, X, will affect the outputs of all the intermediate products used to produce X. This, in turn, affects the outputs of the raw materials, energy inputs, transportation, banking, insurance services, etc. that are tied up with the upstream industries that help to produce X.

This book defines *Leontief's Law* as follows: 'A significant shock to the output of any one good can eventually have upstream effects on the outputs of essentially every other good in the economy.' This represents an integral part of the fourth objective, namely: to illustrate the extreme complexity of the economy by explaining how economic magic and black magic are transmitted throughout the economy downstream via Say's Law and Keynes' Law (the multiplier effect) and upstream via Leontief's Law.

The book addresses each of the economic myths listed immediately below. In some cases, 'back of the envelope' calculations are made in order to get a rough idea about the magnitudes of real-world events. For example, how many jobs have been created indirectly via the net capital inflow that accompanies each year's current account deficit? Another example deals with the extent to which the extra incomes and spending of those who benefit from a higher minimum wage will increase employment throughout the economy. A thoroughly scholarly investigation of each topic and each calculation is beyond the scope of this work. Consequently, a fifth objective is to stimulate research that … goes outside of the box.

1.3   ECONOMIC MYTHS[5]

Myth #1: 'Every job that a Mexican has is one less job for an American.' Equivalently, during the first several decades after World War Two when many women entered the labor market, 'Every job that a woman has is one less job for a man. Immigrants and women take jobs away from American men.'

Such statements are similar to the fact that each new wave of immigrants in the USA was frowned upon by previous immigrants. For example, my Polish grandparents came here in the early 1900s, and Pappy Kovalesky often heard, 'Every job that a Pollock has is one less job for an American.' These statements begin with a tautological statement (if an immigrant or a woman has a job then, of course, an American or a man does not have it) and jump to the macroeconomic conclusion that overall unemployment is positively related to immigration and to the labor force participation rate of women. Nonsense!

Myth #2: 'Every task that a robot performs means less work for people. Eventually, robots will do almost everything, and there simply won't be enough work for humans.' This also jumps from a tautological statement (if a robot does a job, then, of course, a human is not doing it) to a macroeconomic conclusion. This idea creates fear and sells books, but the history of the past few centuries suggests that it is simply a myth.

Myth #3: 'It is folly to believe that workers will benefit much, if at all, from advances in productivity. Trickle-down theory might have worked in the past, but it no longer does.' Those who believe this have data to back them up. The data are terribly flawed!

Myth #4: 'When we buy an imported car (or any foreign made product) then this means that one less car (or product) is made in America. Consequently, imports reduce US output, and employment.' Again, this involves a jump from a tautological statement to a macroeconomic conclusion!

Myth #5: Consistent with #4 is the frequent statement by the media that imports always detract from GDP, because their value is subtracted when the government calculates GDP. This is absolutely false! The people who say this do not understand how GDP is calculated.

Myth #6: 'America imports more than it exports, and this trade deficit exacerbates the loss of jobs from imports.' The truth is that: (a) jobs are lost *directly* as American firms shut down or downsize as a result of excessive imports; but (b) trade balance deficits create jobs *indirectly* by helping the USA grow more rapidly.

Myth #7: 'One reason for our chronic trade balance deficits is cheap foreign labor.' However, the USA imports much from high wage countries such as Canada, Germany, and Japan. Also, its exporting industries pay much higher wage rates than the average in the USA. It is well known among international economic scholars that wage rates affect the composition of the USA's imports, but they have no effect on the overall trade balance.

Myth #8: 'Higher wage rates (when labor productivity has not increased) mean fewer jobs and more unemployment. Firms will hire less labor when it is more costly, especially if there is a large jump in the minimum wage.'

This *microeconomic* conclusion might not be true in the aggregate, because the extra spending by those who benefit from a higher minimum wage will generate employment throughout the economy.

Myth #9: 'Ever since LBJ declared war on poverty, trillions of dollars have been spent on this project with little progress.' There is scholarly research that comes out on both sides of this issue. What is the truth?

One fact for certain is that the government defines and calculates poverty via an absurd method. There are probably tens of millions more poor in the USA than official data imply. Thus, we might have made some progress toward reducing poverty, but official data hide the fact that there could be unbelievably more poor people (by any reasonable standard) than we realize.

Myth #10: 'Decreasing poverty via income redistribution divides the GDP pie more evenly, but the pie will end up smaller (than it would have been without redistribution) because the economy will grow more slowly. Eventually, the poor will be worse off if we grow more slowly.' This statement is widely accepted, but scholarly research and the performance of the Nordic countries suggest that it might simply be a myth.

Myth #11: 'Since a country cannot permanently produce more than its potential output, any Aggregate Demand that exceeds potential output will lead in the long run only to higher prices.' This myth ignores the concept of Economic Hysteresis, which implies that a temporary movement away from equilibrium can permanently alter the equilibrium.

1.4 EVIDENCE OF AND THE DANGER IN NOT KNOWING

1.4.1 Evidence

One reason why economists disagree is that we do not fully understand the complexity of a modern macroeconomy.[6] If we did, then there would not be so many different schools of thought in the realm of macroeconomics. Some of these are: traditional Keynesian Economics; New Keynesian Economics; the Neo-Classical Synthesis; New Classical Economics; Supply Side Economics; New Monetary Theory; and Real Business Cycle theory. Some economists have laughed at traditional Keynesian ideas that are allegedly old-fashioned and not rigorous, and at Supply-Side Economics, which has been called Voodoo Economics.

Real Business Cycle Theory won Finn Kydland and Edward Prescott the 2004 Nobel Prize in economics. This radically different way of thinking has been gaining progressively more disciples, especially in PhD programs. Rational observers of the conflicting macroeconomic theories have to think: (a) 'Which one ... if any ... of these schools of thought is correct?'; (b) 'Is it possible that none of them are totally correct?': and (c) 'Maybe we really don't know!'

The history of scholarly ideas about the causes of the Great Depression provides more evidence consistent with the idea that we do not fully understand the complex nature of the macroeconomy. Fifty or sixty years ago, the list of causes for the Great Depression was shorter than it is now. Since then, we keep coming up with progressively more causes.

Each time this happens, the impression is given that finally we have figured it all out. But perhaps we still do not know all of the causes of the Great Depression. Before the Great Recession of 2007–2009 the list of causes did not include the fact that a Great Depression can occur if banks make too many loans to risky borrowers. However, the financial panic of 2007–2009 brought the world perilously close to Great Depression #2. Finally, to my knowledge, no previous list of causes of an economic depression ever included a pandemic!

1.4.2   The Danger

Somebody once said something like: 'There is only one thing worse than *not knowing*, and that is *thinking you know when you don't*.' Allegedly, the builders of the *Titanic* bragged that finally there was a ship that was unsinkable. We all know what happened. At one point early in my career the powers that be announced that there could never again be a one-day decrease of 11 percent in the price of stocks, as happened at the onset of the Great Depression. But the market went down roughly double that percentage in one day in the fall of 1987.

An excellent example of the danger of not knowing that you don't know relates to how deflation can affect an economy. To explain, any firm can usually sell its entire output if it reduces the prices of its products sufficiently. This microeconomic fact led people in 1929 to believe that a Great Depression could never occur if all firms reduced their prices far enough. Supposedly, this would ensure that all output would be sold; thus, there would be no reason to reduce output, and lay workers off.

However, during the first three years of the Great Depression prices fell significantly, but the economy kept getting worse. Now we know that deflation can cause a Great Depression.[7] This is why American and foreign governments were concerned about the very low inflation rates after the financial crisis of 2007–2008. They believed that an inflation rate of 1 percent could quickly become a negative inflation rate, thereby precipitating an economic collapse. In sum, 'not knowing' probably helped to cause the Great Depression. In recent years, not knowing that import tariffs have little or no positive effect on a country's overall trade balance caused the Trump Administration to risk a potentially disastrous international trade war.

1.5 SOME CAUSES OF ECONOMIC MAGIC AND BLACK MAGIC

When humans have been unable to explain real world events, they have sometimes called it magic. The idea of economic magic is not new. Adam Smith went to great lengths to explain how specialization of labor can generate huge (almost magical) increases in labor productivity. Smith also asserted that self-interest is an important resource in an economy. When self-interest is combined with competition the results can be unbelievably good, i.e., economic magic! Also, John Maynard Keynes believed that the so-called animal spirits of entrepreneurs can have profound (almost magical?) positive or negative effects on an economy.

This book distinguishes between: (a) causes, i.e., the events (real or psychological) that generate good or bad magic, and (b) the transmission mechanism by which a positive or negative cause affects the entire economy. Here is a list of the causes that will be relevant in later chapters.[8]

- Advances in technology and the speed of such advances
- Uncertainty, fear, and panic
- Specialization
- Competition or the lack of it
- Optimism versus (over-confidence or pessimism)
- Bad (wrong) economic theories, i.e., ignorance
- Too much or not enough government regulation
- Corruption
- Bad (biased) data
- Significant changes in labor supply
- Excessive income inequality
- A pandemic
- Rapid increases in the labor supply
- Economic hysteresis

1.6 THE TRANSMISSION MECHANISM

The transmission mechanism involves three economic laws, namely: Say's Law, Keynes' Law, and Leontief's Law. As pointed out above, Say's Law and Keynes' Law, if properly defined, represent the theoretical basis for the multiplier concept. The latter transmits an exogenous spending shock downstream. Leontief's Law, as defined here, is an important new concept that explains how an exogenous output shock is transmitted upstream via the logic involved in an input/output table.

The extreme complexity of a modern economy arises because: (1) each step downstream in the multiplier process initiates a new upstream cause/effect chain via Leontief's Law; and (2) each step upstream via Leontief's Law initiates a new downstream multiplier effect. Chapter 3 elaborates on these important ideas.

1.7   PREVIEW: A SHORT LIST OF SOME OF WHAT FOLLOWS

- Women and immigrants might have an initial negative effect on the employment of American men, but eventually they increase GDP, the average standard of living, and jobs. Traditional thinking does not adequately explain how all of this happens. Economic magic does!
- In spite of many imperfections (especially low national saving rates) and many negative shocks, the US economy performed better during the 30 years prior to COVID-19 than almost every other leading country. More economic magic!
- Imports directly harm some workers and firms, but an increase in foreign competition induces many US firms to shape up. This leads to lower prices, and to dynamic effects such as increased efficiency, higher quality, and many new products that embody advances in technology, e.g., computers, TVs, and cell phones. Decreases in prices and dynamic effects have a positive influence on everyone's standard of living, thereby reducing any harm to specific people. The net effect on many of the so-called losers from trade is uncertain. They might, in general, have a higher standard of living because of international trade, but feel cheated because others have gained much more.
- Balance of trade (or current account) deficits may directly reduce employment, but they indirectly create jobs by helping a country grow more rapidly in two ways. First, they free up domestic resources to produce more capital goods. Second, trade deficits are matched by an inflow of foreign saving and investment funds that help to finance domestic investment. The net effect of trade balance deficits on jobs is unknown.
- An increase in wage rates (without an accompanying advance in productivity) will cause a decrease in jobs directly. This is a *microeconomic* conclusion. However, the increased spending by those with higher incomes serves to create jobs throughout the economy. We have no idea about the net effect.
- The US government determines the poverty threshold income levels (for households of different sizes) by multiplying the cost of food by three. For example, if a single person spends $355 per month on food, then they are classified as poor only if they earn less than $1,065 per month, which amounts to roughly $12,780 per year. If they work 40 hours per week for

52 weeks this annual income amounts to $6.14 per hour. They are not poor if they earn more than $6.14 per hour. *If you buy this nonsense, then I have some ocean front property in Kentucky that I would like to sell you.*

• Scholarly studies have found no consistent relationship between income inequality and economic growth rates for countries. Furthermore, the Nordic countries (who have much less income inequality) have grown more rapidly in recent decades than countries such as the US, Canada, Japan, the UK, Germany, France, and Italy. We simply do not know the effect of income distribution on economic growth rates.

• Fear, panic, and ignorance played major roles in causing the Great Depression. Fear, panic, corruption, and lack of government regulation were important causes of the Great Recession. Finally, fear was much more important than government shut down mandates in the economic harm caused by the COVID-19 pandemic. Economic black magic again.

• The Natural Rate Hypothesis (NRH) implicitly assumes that firms and workers become pessimistic when output temporarily exceeds potential output.[9] That is, it assumes that people believe that a booming economy will not last. This pessimism means that the number and/or size of firms will not go up, and that the labor force participation rate will not increase. If, however, sufficient optimism exists, then both the capital stock and labor supply can increase, thereby generating a higher potential output, and a greater actual output permanently. Macroeconomic hysteresis implies that the NRH need not always be correct.

NOTES

1. Philippon (2019), p. ix.
2. More recently economists have made progress developing theories that take account of psychological factors. See Thaler (2016).
3. Some important contributions of Behavioral Macroeconomics are: (a) Efficiency Wage Theory which helps to explain that involuntary unemployment exists because firms rationally choose to pay a real wage rate that is higher than the labor market clearing wage; (b) why firms choose to increase output initially (and only later raise prices) in response to an increase in aggregate demand; (c) why people save too little for their old age; and (d) why stock prices are much more volatile than the 'fundamental values' for stocks. See Akerlof (2002).
4. Hysteresis refers to the phenomenon whereby a temporary event has a permanent or at least a long lasting influence.
5. This list of myths is not meant to be comprehensive. Moosa (2021) examines other myths, and, hence, can be considered as complementary to this book.
6. There are, of course, other reasons.
7. See Chapter 10 below.
8. This list is not meant to be exhaustive.

9. The NRH maintains that when output temporarily exceeds potential output, then the unemployment rate drops below its 'natural rate'. This puts upward pressure on wage rates, which forces firms to increase prices, thereby reducing aggregate demand and eventually returning output back down to its potential level.

2. Some causes of economic magic and/or black magic

2.1 INTRODUCTION

This chapter briefly explains the causes of economic magic and black magic, as listed in Chapter 1. Later chapters delve more deeply into this topic. Chapter 3 deals with the transmission mechanism by which the effects of any cause spread to every corner of the economy.

2.2 ADVANCES IN TECHNOLOGY AND THEIR SPEED

Advances in technology are a well-known cause of economic development. Joseph Schumpeter, long ago, said that capitalism thrives on innovations.[1] For example, the steam engine revolutionized assembly line production, as well as travel via the sea. Its use in locomotives connected the east and west coasts in the USA. In the process, the transcontinental railways led to the development of hundreds of towns and cities along the way.

The discovery and development of electricity and its uses transformed the world. Computers, cell phones, and the internet are having a profound effect on the world economy, both directly and indirectly. It seems possible that the advances in technology over the last two or three centuries have improved the average standard of living in the world much more than the cumulative improvements over the previous 2,000 years. Advances in technology are, indeed, a cause of economic magic!

However, it is possible for advances in technology to occur too rapidly, thereby generating economic black magic. To take the argument to the extreme, what if advances in technology were so rapid that they resulted in 140 million unemployed, and 10 million people who are working? And suppose that this created a huge gap in standards of living between these 140 million (and their families) and the 10 million (and their families) whose standards of living increased tremendously? I believe that such a situation would be totally unacceptable.

This situation is unrealistic, but hopefully it makes the point! There is conceivably some speed of advances in technology that is too fast. Reasonable people will disagree as to what this speed is, especially because there is a gradual continuum of more and more harm as the speed increases.

If you believe that in reality there is no possibility that technology can advance too fast, then please consider this. In a democratic society, if you get enough losers from any economic event, then (at best) the losers are very likely to form a political coalition.[2] They will elect politicians whose policies appear to be in their self-interest, but could be detrimental to the entire economy, including the losers. Alternatively, as we know so well, the losers might revert to violence!

2.3   UNCERTAINTY AND FEAR[3]

It is useful to define: (a) uncertainty to mean that the future could have good or bad outcomes that are both reasonably possible; and (b) fear to mean uncertainty when the probability of a bad outcome completely dominates. Both uncertainty and fear can be a cause of economic black magic.

2.3.1   Uncertainty

Nobel Prize winner Paul Romer has explained why uncertainty, as defined here, can have a negative effect on the economy.[4] In 2020 he explained that when COVID-19 is under control and the economy is on a path toward normalcy, uncertainty can put a drag on economic recovery. If households and firms, in general, believe that the economy will quickly return to normalcy then: (a) household purchases of durable goods, new houses, expensive vacations, etc. will increase rapidly; and (b) business call-backs of laid-off workers and business efforts to increase productive capacity will be rapid. On the other hand, just the opposite will occur if households and firms, in general, believe that the economy will return to normalcy slowly.

What happens if there is complete uncertainty about the speed of recovery back toward normalcy? The most likely result is that households will hold back on big time purchases, and firms will be slow in calling back workers and/ or expanding. Few households want to risk being stuck with a huge monthly mortgage or car payment if things turn out badly. Firms do not want to have a newly constructed facility sitting idle. In sum, uncertainty can be a cause of economic black magic.

2.3.2   Fear

A story
When I was 12 years old, I played on a kids football team. I vividly recall one day when we were at one end of the field warming up for a big game. One of my teammates looked at our opponents at the other end of the field and said, 'Oh my God, look at them; they are giants!' Most of us stopped warming up momentarily to stare in disbelief. Somebody said, 'We are gonna get killed!' Our coach quickly saw what was going on and his stern response was 'Don't look at them! Do you understand? Don't look at them!' He knew that extreme fear could mean that we would not play well!

Fear can generate the bad result for an economy that is feared. The stock market crash in the fall of 1929 and newspaper pictures of people jumping out of the windows of tall buildings created much fear. Consumer purchases of durable goods decreased immediately thereafter, thereby exacerbating an economic downturn that had begun in the summer of 1929.[5] Also, there is a consensus that a decrease in the US money supply of more than 30 percent from 1929–1932 helped to cause the Great Depression. A scholarly paper by Mitchener and Richardson concludes that the money supply decreased primarily because of fear.[6]

As we know, generally the money supply expands when banks make more loans and contracts when banks make fewer loans. In 1929 and the early 1930s fear prompted people to run to their bank to withdraw funds before the bank went under. Thus, banks had fewer funds to lend. In addition, thousands of banks were forced to close, and banks that are closed do not make loans. Finally, fear prompted the banks that survived to build up excess reserves, which meant that they made fewer loans. The decrease in bank loans caused aggregate demand to fall, thereby helping to generate the Great Depression.

A scholarly study by Goolsbee and Syverson concluded that the fear generated by the COVID-19 pandemic caused a decrease in spending, output, and jobs that exceeded the negative effects from shutdowns ordered by state and local governments.[7] These researchers found that only seven percentage points of the decrease in business activity can be attributed to legal mandates. The rest of the decline came from consumers voluntarily avoiding stores, movies, restaurants, travel, etc.

2.4   SPECIALIZATION

Adam Smith explained how specialization can create economic magic via a detailed example of pin production in England, in and around 1776. He pointed out that making a pin involved about eighteen distinct operations. Furthermore, he had observed businesses wherein ten men could make about

48 thousand pins a day, whereas without any specialization they each could not make more than 20 pins per day.[8]

Specialization can be a cause of economic magic by increasing labor productivity tremendously. However, it can also generate black magic because it makes everyone interdependent. The latter is obvious at the individual level. We depend on others to produce almost everything we consume. Similarly, everyone depends on others to purchase the good or service that they produce. When something creates a negative shock to an economy, everything goes downhill faster because of specialization.

International specialization via comparative advantage increases the output of all countries; thus, world output goes up. The problem is that some people in each country might be worse off in an absolute sense. More importantly, as pointed out in Chapter 1, many others are worse off in a relative sense. International trade might make them better off but much less than the big gainers from trade. Consequently, they feel left behind.

International specialization creates interdependence among nations. One reason for this is that the production of many, if not most, products involves an international supply chain. For example, Nobel Prize winner Milton Friedman pointed out long ago that the production of a pencil involved: (a) graphite from Sri Lanka, (b) an eraser made from Indonesian rapeseed oil and sulfur chloride, (c) wood from Oregon, and (d) assembly in Wilkes-Barre Pennsylvania.[9] He did not mention the fact that these inputs have to be transported at each stage in the production process, and then the pencils transported to retail stores.

Furthermore, international specialization can potentially create bottlenecks and shortages of products that are crucial. One example deals with N95 face masks at the beginning of the pandemic. Two other examples are antibiotics and computer chips. A shortage of the latter increased new and used car prices so much that in early 2022 some three-year-old used cars were selling at or higher than their new-car sticker price. Clearly, there is an optimum degree of specialization for a country, and I strongly suspect that the USA has exceeded that optimum.

2.5   COMPETITION OR THE LACK OF IT

A story
From the end of World War Two until the early 1970s, American auto firms faced almost no foreign competition. I believe that this allowed US cars to be built with very poor quality. When I bought my first new car in 1963, I opened the trunk and to my surprise I saw several nuts and bolts as well as a few odd-shaped pieces of metal. When I asked the dealership what these were, the reply was: 'Oh, those are simply the parts to the car that were not built into

the car when it was moving along the assembly line. They throw them into the trunk when the car exits the factory. Don't worry! The car is running great, so probably these parts are not important!'

American made cars no longer go out of the factory with nuts, bolts and small parts missing. Why? A good candidate is that foreign competition forced the American firms to shape up. In addition, Chapter 1 mentioned that scholarly evidence suggests that foreign competition has prompted many firms to become more efficient and to innovate more rapidly. In sum, competition works like magic for an economy. The lack of competition can kill an economy.

The divergent economic performances of Poland and Ukraine in the two decades before 2020 represent an excellent example of the importance of competition. Each country's GDP was close to $100 billion in 1990, but by 2018 Poland's GDP had skyrocketed to $585.7 billion while the GDP in Ukraine was a measly $130.8 billion. According to Nobel Prize winner Jean Tirole:

> In Poland, EU competition has made it possible to prevent monopolies from forming ... whereas in Ukraine the opposite happened ... partly because of political corruption.[10]

Thomas Philippon convincingly argues that competition in the USA has decreased significantly in recent years, especially in the telecommunication and airline industries. He bases this conclusion on data associated with concentration ratios, prices, and profit markups.[11] Similarly, Faccio and Zingales say that US consumers would gain $65 billion per year if American prices in the telecommunication industry were as low as in Germany.[12] The data driving these conclusions are impressive.

2.6   OPTIMISM VERSUS PESSIMISM

Optimism about the economy makes households more willing to spend, especially on consumer durables and houses. Pessimism has just the opposite effect. This is not rocket science. However, I believe that optimism/pessimism represent unbelievably powerful causes of economic magic or black magic. In order to develop this idea we must first digress.

2.6.1   Conventional Thinking: The Natural Rate Hypothesis

Conventional thinking in macroeconomics, as described in almost all principles of macroeconomics textbooks, is as follows. Any increase in aggregate demand that occurs when the economy is producing its potential output will, in the long run, have no effect on output or employment. It will just generate higher prices, because an economy cannot produce more than its potential output in the long run. The unemployment rate that exists when actual output equals potential output is called the natural rate of unemployment.

In sum, a country cannot persistently produce more than its potential output, and it cannot persistently keep unemployment lower than its natural rate of unemployment.[13] This seems like it has to be true, but it ignores the possibility of economic hysteresis, and (as pointed out in Chapter 1) it implicitly assumes that eventually people become pessimistic when the economy is booming.

2.6.2   Potential Output

Potential output depends positively on technology, the labor supply, and the capital stock. In the world of macroeconomics, potential output is *not* the absolutely all-out maximum that a country can produce. Rather, it refers to the maximum *sustainable* output. Many firms will temporarily produce more than they care to in order to satisfy good customers, or to get new customers. Potential output can be thought of as the sum of the output of all firms if every one of them is producing the output that maximizes its profits. US firms in the manufacturing sector tell us that this occurs at roughly 80 percent of their maximum, i.e., when their capacity utilization rate is around .80.

2.6.3   Pessimism, Optimism, and the Natural Rate Hypothesis

The Natural Rate Hypothesis (NRH) says that when firms temporarily produce beyond their optimum capacity utilization rate this increases costs per unit of output, thereby prompting firms eventually to raise prices. The latter puts a damper on aggregate demand and eventually returns the economy to its potential output.

An implicit assumption in the NRH is that firms and workers eventually become pessimistic when the economy is booming. That is, firms do not expand and new firms do not arise. In addition, people do not give up their welfare or disability payments (even though jobs are plentiful) because they believe that any new job might be short-lived. If, however, sufficient optimism exists then a booming economy can stimulate an increase in the capital stock and labor supply, thereby increasing potential output.

It is true that an economy cannot permanently produce more than its potential output. However, a temporary increase in output beyond potential output can permanently increase potential output. Consequently, it is possible for actual output to be permanently higher. This represents an example of economic hysteresis, to which we now turn.

2.7 POSITIVE AND NEGATIVE ECONOMIC HYSTERESIS

Take an iron bar and loop an insulated wire around it. If you pass an electric current through the wire, the iron bar will become magnetized. After the current is turned off, the magnetism is not completely lost. The current was temporary, but it had a lasting effect. This phenomenon is called hysteresis.[14]

Economists have used the concept of 'hysteresis' to explain the investment behavior of firms, including foreign direct investment in the USA, the response of imports to exchange rate variations, and how temporary increases in the unemployment rate can alter a country's natural rate of unemployment.[15] Unfortunately, the concept of economic hysteresis has not found its way into mainstream macroeconomic thinking.

In recent decades, the US economy has been strongly influenced both by positive and negative hysteresis. For example, GDP grew steadily for 120 months during the 1990s. Then it increased for almost 130 months before the coronavirus attacked. Both of these expansions occurred with very slow increases in prices. These facts run contrary to the NRH, but are consistent with the concept of positive economic hysteresis, i.e., economic magic!

On the other hand, a severe economic downturn, as occurred during the Great Recession of 2007–2009, causes massive unemployment, increases debts, and generates much fear and uncertainty. Chapter 11 argues that the Great Recession generated negative economic hysteresis in the form of very slow economic growth for roughly four years.

This, in turn, led some economists to conclude that the 'good old days' of rapid economic growth were gone forever. In addition, the slow growth rates created the myth that the economic policies of Obama killed economic growth, when (in fact) over the last three years of the Obama Administration, the economy's performance equaled that of Trump's first three years.

Chapter 12 maintains that COVID-19 led to government policies and actions by firms and workers that have created negative economic hysteresis in the form of a very high inflation rate. For example, allegedly, roughly 200,000 businesses closed during the first eight months after the virus attacked. This decreased the useful capital stock, i.e., businesses that are shut down do not produce. Potential output declines if the useful capital stock decreases.[16]

In addition, in the first year or so of the pandemic the number of people who retired was more than one million greater than usual. This decrease in the labor supply also reduced potential output. COVID-19 also created bottlenecks in the supply chain, most notably via computer chips. Finally, the actions of Congress and the Federal Reserve increased the money supply unbelievably fast, thereby sowing the seeds of high inflation. COVID-19 appears to be under control for now, but the inflationary consequences of the negative economic hysteresis (e.g., a lower potential output and rapid increase in the money supply) that it generated could possibly persist for many years.

2.8   OVER-CONFIDENCE

The possibility of people becoming overly optimistic and overly confident is real, and it has led to dire consequences (*black magic*). For example, the average value over roughly 100 years for the Standard and Poor Price (P) Earnings (E) ratio (P/E) is 15.54. Nobel Laureate Robert Shiller prefers a cyclically adjusted version of this with an average value of 16.6. Near the end of the dot-com speculative bubble in the 1990s, the Shiller's P/E peaked around 42. Both Alan Greenspan (Chair of the Fed at that time) and Shiller called this 'irrational exuberance'. The speculative bubble in internet stocks eventually burst, taking some stocks down from roughly $100 per share to less than $1, and inducing an economic recession.

Another example of over-optimism eventually harming the economy relates to housing prices. Case, Shiller and Thompson found that from 2000 to 2005 (when the prices of houses were rising rapidly) homeowners expected housing prices to go up annually by 10 percent or more for another 10 years.[17] Such over-optimism fueled the housing bubble that ultimately burst when housing prices decreased in 2006 for the first time since World War Two. This led to: (a) the so-called subprime financial crisis of 2007–2009, (b) the Great Recession of 2007–2009, and (c) many years of slow economic growth for the US economy. Economic black magic!

2.9   BAD (WRONG) ECONOMIC THEORIES OR JUST PLAIN IGNORANCE

Ignorance with regard to how an economy functions can also have very negative consequences. Chapter 1 explained how faulty economic thinking about deflation might have helped to create the Great Depression. Another example deals with the fact the Herbert Hoover's administration increased tax rates in 1932. Allegedly, Hoover's advisors told him that people were losing confidence in the government, because the Great Depression had lowered tax revenues and created a government budget deficit.

Consequently, the Hoover Administration increased taxes to balance the budget and restore confidence in the government. At that time aggregate demand was too low and was falling. Higher taxes meant lower after-tax incomes and a decrease in spending. This made the Great Depression worse. Clearly, ignorance can be a cause of economic black magic!

2.10 GOVERNMENT REGULATION AND CORRUPTION

Most people would agree that too much or too little government regulation can harm an economy. At one point it seemed necessary to regulate the airline industry in order to ensure that the USA had a viable fleet that could be commandeered in times of war. However, this kept prices artificially high. The Airline Deregulation Act of 1978 phased out government controls on routes and ticket prices. In the decade or so after this, airline fares per passenger mile came down approximately 50 percent while prices of other products increased significantly.

Ostensibly in an attempt to protect railroads, the Motor Carrier Act of 1935 gave the government authority to regulate the trucking industry by imposing restrictive, complicated rules about pricing and territory. The law gave the Interstate Commerce Commission (ICC) the power to determine which companies were allowed to be interstate carriers, what they would haul, and the fees they charged. The Motor Carrier Act of 1980, signed by President Carter on 1 July of that year, ended this stifling regulation. In the next ten years the number of trucking firms roughly doubled, and trucking rates fell significantly. This reduced the prices of everything carried by trucks and saved consumers billions of dollars per year.

Many businesspeople complained that the Obama Administration burdened them with too many regulations and too much bureaucratic red tape, especially when a firm wanted to expand. Political conservatives believe that over-regulation was partially to blame for the fact that the USA grew very slowly for several years after the Great Recession of 2007–2009. However, Chapter 4 will show that in the last three years of the Obama Administration, the economy performed as well (with all those terrible regulations) as it did in the first three years of the Trump Administration (with many fewer regulations).

Not enough regulation is at the opposite extreme! This can also be a cause of economic black magic. In 1999 the government rescinded a portion of the 1933 Glass-Steagall Act that regulates banks. Chapter 10 suggests that this was one of the underlying causes of the financial crisis of 2007–2009, which almost took the world into Great Depression #2.

Turn next to the topic of corruption and its effect on an economy. Surprisingly, scholarly studies have not found a consistent relationship between corruption and economic performance as measured by economic growth rates. For example, Mauro, as well as Blackburn et al., find that increases in corruption serve to reduce economic growth.[18] Contrastingly, Meon and Weill (2010) as well as Kato and Sato (2015) conclude just the opposite, i.e., higher corruption increases growth rates.[19] These puzzling results will not be explored here, but they are another example of 'we really do not know'! However, Chapter 11 suggests that corruption contributed to the Great Recession of 2007–2009.

2.11   BAD (OR BIASED) ECONOMIC DATA

There has been a well-known upward bias in the Consumer Price Index, CPI, for many decades. Why this is true will be addressed in Chapter 6. What is important here is that this bias makes it seem like the economy is not functioning in a manner that helps the average worker when labor productivity increases. Political liberals use this distortion of the truth as hard evidence that the US economy needs to be altered drastically (*black magic*).

Chapter 1 pointed out that the government calculates the value for the poverty threshold income in a manner that most reasonable people would laugh at. These faulty data make it seem as though there are millions of fewer poor people than actually exist. It is not unreasonable to believe that this affects government policies to reduce poverty (*black magic*).

2.12   RAPID INCREASES IN LABOR SUPPLY[20]

A country's potential output depends on technology, the labor supply and the capital stock (structures and equipment). Consequently, immigration and women entering the labor force are good for an economy in that they increase potential output, i.e., economic magic. However, microeconomic theory suggests a large increase in the labor supply can conceivably cause unemployment to rise, and/or can reduce the equilibrium wage rate for certain types of labor. If so, then a rapid increase in labor supply can conceivably be a cause of economic black magic. However, in general this does not appear to have occurred.

How do new workers find jobs without always causing higher unemployment rates and/or lower wage rates for previous workers? The standard answer is that a growing economy needs more workers. Advances in technology and capital accumulation have been positive in the USA almost every year, thereby causing economic growth and creating jobs. Personally, I suspect there is much more to it than this. Is it possible that a large number of entrants into the labor force somehow stimulates economic growth? That is, does reverse causation occur? Chapter 4 explores this possibility.

NOTES

1.   Schumpeter (1942).
2.   The so-called losers need not be worse off in an absolute sense, i.e., their stand-ard of living need not have gone down. Advances in technology might increase

their standard of living, but not nearly as much as it has for others. All that is necessary is for them to feel left behind in a relative sense.

3. A discussion of panic is postponed until Chapters 10 and 11 which address the Great Depression and the Great Recession.
4. See Seib (2020).
5. See Romer (1990).
6. Mitchener and Richardson (2020).
7. Goolsbee and Syverson (2020).
8. Smith (1937 [1776]), pp. 4–5.
9. Friedman (1962), p. 109.
10. Tirole (2017), p. 357.
11. Philippon (2019).
12. Faccio and Zingales (2017).
13. This is called the Natural Rate Hypothesis (NRH) and it was an important component of the research of Nobel Prize winner Milton Friedman.
14. See Dixit (1992).
15. Two excellent references on economic hysteresis are: Cross (1993) and Blanchard and Summers (1988).
16. The idea of useful capital stock is not part of conventional thinking. It is my understanding that typically calculations of potential output implicitly include all of the existing capital stock. All definitions are arbitrary, but it seems reasonable to define potential output as depending, in part, only on those structures (factories, warehouses, etc.) and equipment that are owned by an active business. This would be equivalent to the fact that discouraged workers are not counted as part of the labor supply when we calculate potential output.
17. Case, Shiller and Thompson (2012).
18. Mauro (1995), and Blackburn, Bose and Haque (2006).
19. Meon and Weill (2010), and Kato and Sato (2015).
20. Excessive income inequality and the pandemic as causes of economic black magic are addressed in Chapters 7 and 12.

3.   The magic and black magic transmission mechanism

3.1   INTRODUCTION

Chapter 3 explains how economic magic and/or black magic are transmitted throughout the economy. Macroeconomics has traditionally focused on how changes in aggregate demand lead to more or less income for others, who then spend more or less, etc. This so-called multiplier effect transmits a shock to the economy *downstream*. This one-sided perspective on the transmission of economic shocks followed naturally from the fact that traditionally macroeconomic theories assume that only one all-purpose good exists.

The pandemic made it perfectly clear that economic shocks are also transmitted *upstream*. When people stayed home and bought less of some product X, this affected all those who produced the nuts and bolts, intermediate products, and raw materials used to make X. For example, when a restaurant in Cartersville GA closed this affected: (a) local farmers; (b) table-cloth suppliers; (c) a liquor store; (d) credit card companies; a bank; and many others.[1]

Chapter 1 pointed out that the transmission mechanism includes: (a) Say's Law; (b) Keynes' Law; and (c) a new concept called Leontief's Law. These interact in a manner such that a significant increase (or decrease) in the output of any one good generates an unbelievably complex series of cause–effect chains that can eventually affect every sector of an economy.

3.2   SAY'S LAW

In 1803 the French economist Jean-Baptiste Say discovered and explained an important truth about economies:

> It is worthwhile to remark that a product is no sooner created than it, from that instant, affords a market for other products to the full extent of its own value.[2]

In 1936 the English economist John Maynard Keynes stated Say's Law in a manner that could easily be attacked, i.e., he set up a straw man. His words were:

> From the time of Say and Ricardo [the latter came up with the theory of comparative advantage] the classical economists have taught that supply creates its own demand.[3]

Ever since Keynes misrepresented it, Say's Law is usually stated as 'supply creates its own demand'. This straw man has been taken to imply that the income earned by the workers who produce any product, X, will automatically generate a demand for X that is sufficient to buy all of it. Clearly, this is not what Say had in mind.

Productive activity almost always generates income for those who produce. Workers get paid; suppliers of raw materials and parts get paid; and profits are earned. For example, assume that a new Chevy sells for $30,000. The car salesperson will get a commission, say, $500. The Chevy dealership will earn a profit, say $2,500. That leaves $27,000 to be paid to General Motors. GM, in turn, will use this $27,000 to pay its workers, the suppliers of parts, its debtors, and its stockholders. When GM pays all its bills to suppliers, they, in turn, pay their workers and suppliers. Theoretically, the entire $30,000 ends up going to someone as income.[4]

Consequently, when a $30,000 car is produced, this creates $30,000 of income in the economy. If all income is spent, then the supply of a $30,000 car will generate a demand of $30,000 for goods and services. Naturally, the $30,000 demand for goods and services would be for many products, not just Chevy cars. This is what Say's quote (above) tells us.[5]

Some output will not be bought (even though people have enough income to do so) if people save. *Consequently, all saving must be borrowed by someone and spent in order for all output to be bought.* This is a fundamental principle of macroeconomics. Typically, in well-functioning credit markets, interest rates (and credit standards) will adjust so that essentially all saving is borrowed and spent.

There are two reasons why some saving might not be borrowed and spent. People might stash some of their savings away in a safe, a piggy bank, or under the bed mattress. This hoarding of money happens often when fear runs rampant in an economy (*black magic*). In addition, even if all saving finds its way to banks, bankers might be reluctant to lend all of it if they fear that borrowers might not repay. When banks are afraid to lend this reduces spending and often induces an economy to spiral downward.

The term Say's Law will be used here to refer to the statement: 'Supply creates incomes which can potentially buy an equal value of output.' The important idea here is that production (supply) generates income and some demand.

3.3   KEYNES' LAW

Another aspect of the macroeconomy that helps to spread the effects of any initial positive or negative shock to the economy is Keynes' Law. In its simplest form, Keynes' Law is just the opposite of Say's Law, namely: 'Demand creates its own supply'. In other words, a demand for some product X will induce someone to supply X, provided that it is profitable to do so.

An example that is consistent with Keynes' Law deals with the development of mass production techniques for cars, and the eventual building of an extensive network of highways in the USA. These led to an increased demand for gas stations, road-side fast food restaurants, and relatively inexpensive motels. It did not take long for businesses to start supplying these. Similarly, when electric cars catch on, we will see tens of thousands of charging stations being constructed.

Some examples of Keynes' Law deal with illegal activities. One of these is related to the prohibition period in the USA, 1920–1933. Clearly, many people wanted to consume alcoholic beverages, and this made it profitable for someone to supply them. More recently, people want to use illegal drugs. The government spends about $50 billion per year on drug law enforcement, apparently to little avail. The demand for drugs has created supply (Keynes' Law) even at the risk faced by suppliers of going to jail or being killed by other drug dealers.

Another example of Keynes' Law deals with the fact that driving over the 4.3 mile long Chesapeake Bay Bridge is terrifying for some drivers. The probability of driving off the bridge is minuscule, but 12 people have done so since it opened in 1964, most recently a truck driver in February 2017. This proved to be fatal for ten of them. Prior to 2007 the Maryland Transportation Authority drove nervous drivers across the bridge. When they stopped doing this there was clearly a demand for such a service, and currently three different small businesses do so (in your car) for a relatively small fee. Keynes' Law works!

There are two versions of Keynes' Law. The first relates to the situation when Keynes published his famous book during the Great Depression. At that time there was excess capacity in essentially all industries. Hence, it was easy to accept the idea that if people demand more of a product in such a situation, then it would be produced. We will refer to this as the Weak Version of Keynes' Law.

The second version of Keynes' Law deals with the hypothetical situation wherein aggregate demand increases when an economy is initially producing its potential output. Economists have disagreed as to whether Keynes' Law holds in this case. Chapter 2 explained the Natural Rate Hypothesis, NRH. For review, the NRH maintains that an increase in aggregate demand might induce firms to temporarily increase output beyond the profit maximizing level. However, in the long run the firms will increase prices; hence, aggregate demand will decrease, and output will return to its previous level, e.g., potential output.

As pointed out in Chapter 2, the concept of economic hysteresis suggests that this scenario might not always hold. Existing firms might expand their productive capacity and/or new firms might be created when the economy is booming, i.e., when output exceeds potential output. If so, then an increase in aggregate demand will increase potential output and, thus, actual output, i.e., economic hysteresis. We will refer to this as the Strong Version of Keynes' Law.

BOX 3.1 A DIGRESSION

If you can accept the idea that a booming economy might induce firms to expand their productive capacity and/or for new firms to arise, then this section can be skipped with no loss in continuity. Otherwise, read on. All of the discussion here relates to the case where an economy is producing its potential output and then aggregate demand increases.

Objection #1

One argument against the existence of the Strong Version of Keynes' Law is that it holds at the microeconomic level, but not for the entire economy. That is: (a) if any one firm increases the output of a good that is in high demand, then that firm will have to decrease the output of other goods, i.e., no net increase in output; and (b) any investment for expansion of existing firms or the entry of new firms to produce a product in high demand will mean a decrease in investment in other industries.

Allegedly, two reasons exist for these assertions. First, from a financial perspective, firms must finance investment in new facilities by using saving, either their own or borrowing other people's savings. If aggregate demand increases, then there will be less saving in the economy, not more. Thus, the Strong Version of Keynes' Law is (allegedly) not valid.

Reply #1

Objection #1 is not valid for two reasons. In an open economy the extra funds to finance new and/or expanding firms can be obtained by borrowing internationally. For many decades, America has used hundreds of billions of dollars in foreign saving each year to help finance domestic investment. Furthermore, the government (via the banking system) can create money to finance domestic investment.

Objection #2

The second perspective deals with real output. Critics of the Strong Version of Keynes' Law say that when an economy is producing its potential output, then it cannot produce more capital goods (that are needed for new firms and/or expanding firms) unless it produces fewer consumer goods. However, an increase in aggregate demand is almost certain to include a demand for more consumer goods. The economy cannot produce more consumer goods and more capital goods simultaneously. Hence, again, the Strong Version of Keynes' Law, allegedly, is not valid.

Reply #2

Again, this logic is not true for an open economy. Imports can increase relative to exports. This will give an economy the opportunity to have more capital goods without reducing consumption. It can import capital goods, or it can import consumer goods, thereby freeing domestic resources to produce more productive facilities and equipment. As pointed out earlier, one important idea in this book is that trade balance deficits have helped the US economy grow faster and create jobs.[6]

3.4   LEONTIEF'S LAW

> You could not remove a single grain of sand from its place without thereby ... changing something throughout all parts of the immeasurable whole.[7]

The third macroeconomic concept that helps to propagate economic magic or black magic follows from the input–output table developed by the 1973 Nobel Laureate, Wassily Leontief. This has implications for an economy that are conceptually similar to the so-called 'butterfly effect' in physics, weather forecasting, chaos theory, etc.

As pointed out in Chapter 1, Leontief's Law is defined here as follows: 'A significant change in the output of any one product, X, will necessitate a change in the upstream output of all goods that are used directly and indirectly (including raw materials, transportation, finance, insurance, etc.) to produce X.'

The 'butterfly effect' refers to the hypothetical idea that a butterfly flapping its wings in the Amazon jungle can conceivably initiate a chain of events that eventually creates a hurricane or a tornado thousands of miles away. Among other things, this story suggests that everything is affected by everything else, at least with respect to the weather, and that small initial disturbances can generate huge final effects.

In the 1950s the meteorologist and mathematician Edward Lorenz (1917–2008) was, allegedly, in a hurry to duplicate a weather experiment that used a mathematical model. Thus, he entered the initial condition 0.506 instead of the previously used 0.506127. The surprising result was a significant change in the model's prediction of the weather. A tiny change in the initial conditions had a significant long-term effect. Lorenz later came up with the butterfly analogy to illustrate his findings. Eventually, Lorenz was instrumental in developing Chaos Theory.[8]

An input–output table shows how much of each product is needed to produce every other product. The basic idea of an input–output table can be understood via a simple example. Suppose that there is a desire to significantly increase the output of motor vehicles in an economy. This will require a greater output for tires, windshields, engines, seats, etc. These, in turn, require more rubber, glass, steel, leather, cloth, etc. More steel increases the need for iron ore, and coke. The latter, in turn, will require more heavy equipment. Furthermore, transporting the iron ore and coke to the steel mills, and transporting the new steel that is produced, will necessitate more trucks and trains. The same ideas hold for glass, rubber, leather, etc.

In sum, increasing the output of one good, motor vehicles, necessitates increases in the output of many other goods that are used directly or indirectly to produce them. In a Leontief input–output table a substantial increase or decrease in the output of any product will eventually affect the upstream output of every other product. Say's Law and Keynes' Law transmit shocks to an economy downstream as incomes and spending change. Leontief's Law transmits economic shocks upstream.

What is crucial here is that every upstream change in output via Leontief's Law starts a new cause–effect chain downstream via Say's and Keynes' Law. For example, if fewer tires are produced because of a decrease in the output of motor vehicles, then incomes and spending decrease for those who work in the tire industry. This decrease in spending reduces the output of many consumer goods and services, which then starts a new cause–effect chain upstream in the industries that produce what tire makers typically buy.

3.5   THE TRANSMISSION MECHANISM SUMMARIZED

In sum, Say's Law and Keynes' Law transmit any initial change in economic activity downstream. Higher output for, say, product X creates more income in the X industry and the likelihood of more spending on many other products (Say's Law). The latter, in turn, leads to an increase in incomes for the store owners (and workers) from whom people buy. These extra incomes, in turn, create another round of increased spending. Ultimately, incomes and spending go up cumulatively by much more than any initial increase.

Say's Law and Keynes' Law together provide the basis for the so-called 'multiplier concept' that appears in essentially all principles of macroeconomics textbooks. But this is only a part of the reason why any initial cause of economic magic and/or black magic eventually affects the entire economy.

To repeat for emphasis, Leontief's Law deals with the upstream effects of any initial change in output. In order for the output of product X to go up, there need to be more nuts and bolts and intermediate products that are used to produce X. This, in turn, requires an increase in the raw materials used to make the nuts and bolts, and intermediate products. Producing these will increase jobs and incomes even more.

In addition, as upstream outputs rise via Leontief's Law, Say's Law becomes operative again. The higher incomes earned upstream from the production of more inputs for X will increase the demand for many (mostly consumer) goods. Keynes' Law ensures that someone will produce more of these 'many goods'. Then Leontief's Law becomes relevant again. Each additional unit of 'many goods' requires output to increase for the nuts and bolts, intermediate products, and raw materials needed for 'many goods'.

The Strong Version of Keynes' Law requires an increase in productive capacity to satisfy (produce) all of the increases in aggregate demand. Among other things this will stimulate construction of new or expanding facilities as well as the production of the machines and tools that are used in these facilities. This, in turn, increases jobs and incomes in construction and machine tool industries.

Furthermore, at essentially every step along the way, firms and stores need to finance their projects, their inventories, and payments to labor, because workers get paid and intermediate products must be paid for long before a product is sold and generates revenue. Hence, jobs and incomes go up in the finance industry. Similar logic suggests that Leontief's Law means that insurance services will also expand.

Each upstream and downstream cause–effect chain in the transmission process is essentially endless, and each step along the way initiates another upstream and downstream cause–effect chain. Eventually, every aspect of an economy (industries, firms, workers, families, etc.) can conceivably be affected by an initial cause of economic magic or black magic.

3.6   AN ANALOGY

Analogies are often useful for understanding a complex idea. Here is one that might help. Suppose there is a circular pond that is 50 feet in diameter and everywhere five feet deep. This pond has a surface area of 1963.5 square feet, and a volume of 9817.5 cubic feet.[9] Also, assume that there is no wind to cause ripples in the water. If you drop a heavy round rock (a sphere) that is one foot in diameter straight down and it lands precisely in the middle of the pond, it will set off ripples that go in all directions.

Eventually, the ripples will hit every inch of the shore. Also, every square inch of the surface water will be affected, even though the rock initially hit only a trivial percentage (0.7854 square feet) of the pond's surface.[10] If the heavy rock falls straight down, it will directly disturb only 3.927 cubic feet of water,[11] but every drop of the 9817.5 cubic feet of water in the pond (not just the surface water) will move. An economy is similar. Any nontrivial disturbance can affect absolutely every nook and cranny of an economy.

Furthermore, assume that some water splashes out of the pond permanently when the ripples hit the shoreline. After everything settles down, the depth of the pond will be permanently lower. This represents an example of hysteresis, i.e., a temporary shock has a permanent long run effect.

NOTES

1.   Simon (2020), p. B1.
2.   Say (1803), pp. 138–139. A copy of the original page on which this quote appears can be found on page 1 of: http://la.utexas.edu/users/hcleaver/368/368Say TreatiseBk1Ch15table.pdf.
3.   Keynes (1936), p. 18. Material within square brackets added for clarity.
4.   Two complications make this statement only an approximation in the real world. If GM places, say, $500 of the $27,000 into a depreciation account, then initially this does not represent income for anybody. Also, the US government adds the sales tax on the new Chevy, say $1,500, to its price when it calculates the contribution to GDP from the new Chevy. Initially, this $1,500 does not become income for anyone. It goes to the government.
5.   If the government taxes away some of this $30,000 then the demand for goods and services by people will be reduced.
6.   The Strong Version of Keynes' Law is consistent with an idea by Nobel Prize winner Paul Samuelson, called the 'accelerator effect'. This was an integral part of his theory of business cycles, wherein he assumed that increases in a country's income and/or consumption would induce firms to invest and expand productive capacity. See Samuelson (1939).

7.   Fichte (1800), as quoted in (2017), 'The Butterfly Effect: everything you need
      to know about this powerful mental model', *Farnam Street*, https://www.fs.blog/
      2017/08/the-butterfly-effect/.
8.   The underlying idea of the butterfly effect existed as a proverb in fourteenth-century
      England and thirteenth-century Germany, e.g., 'The lack of one horseshoe nail
      could be inconsequential, or it could indirectly cause the loss of a war.'
9.   The radius is 25 feet, and $\prod(25)^2 = 3.1416 \times 625 = 1963.5$ sq ft. The volume is 5
      $\times$ 1963.5 = 9 817.5 cubic ft.
10. $3.1416 \times (1/2)^2 = 0.7854$.
11. $5 \times 0.7854 = 3.927$.

4. The proof of the pudding

4.1 INTRODUCTION

Many people are familiar with the saying, 'the proof of the pudding is in the eating'. The mythical statements in Chapter 1 imply that the US economy has been harmed by imports, trade deficits, immigration, women entering the labor force, computers, and robots. However, by any reasonable standard and by comparison with other leading countries, the US economy performed well over the 30 or 40 years before the coronavirus pandemic. The pudding tasted great! It seems like economic magic was at work.

Then COVID-19 attacked the world, and the US economy quickly collapsed into what many feared might be Great Depression #2. All of a sudden, the complex interaction of every sector of our economy that created economic magic for many decades was now at work via black magic. The pudding tasted like poison.

This chapter first discusses women, immigrants, and jobs, and points out that conventional thinking does not adequately explain how and why increases in the labor supply typically do not create unemployment. Then the chapter addresses Technology, computers, robots, and international trade. Finally, the chapter examines: (a) US pre-virus data on GDP, economic growth, inflation, unemployment, business cycles, and standards of living; and (b) US economic performance compared to that of other leading countries.

4.2 WOMEN, IMMIGRANTS, AND JOBS

4.2.1 Women

If every job a woman has is one less job for a man, then how can this tautological statement be reconciled with the following facts? In December 1949 there were 16.33 million women in the US labor force and the unemployment rate for men was 3.4 percent. From that date through December 1969 the number of women in the labor force increased by almost 14 million. However, the unemployment rate for men in December 1969 was only 3.0 percent.[1]

In the 1840s and 1850s, as the industrial revolution and factory work took hold in the USA, more women went to work outside the home. In 1840, only

10 percent of all adult women were in the labor force. Over the next ten years the figure rose to 15 percent; that represented a 50 percent increase in just one decade. In 1950 the labor force participation rate for women in the USA was about 33 percent. This increased steadily, especially from 1975 to the late 1990s, with a maximum of close to 60 percent.

As of 2019 there were roughly as many women workers in the USA as there were men, and women are entering the labor force with more formal education than men. Furthermore, women produce roughly 40 percent of the USA's GDP each year. This amounts to more than $20 billion worth of output per day. The average standard of living in the USA would be 40 percent lower without women in the labor force. To get a feel for this, imagine that your income, and/or your family's income, suddenly went down to 60 percent of its current magnitude. That is roughly what would be true if there were no women in the labor force.

4.2.2   Immigrants

Essentially all Americans are descendants of immigrants. The Miller side of me came from Germany, and (as mentioned in Chapter 1) Grandma and Pappy Kovalesky immigrated from Poland in the early 1900s. The foreign-born share of the US population has increased for decades, and especially rapidly since about 1970. Foreign born was almost 45 million (almost 14 percent) in 2018.[2] Furthermore, as of 2019 about 17 percent of all workers in the USA were immigrants.

If recent immigrants took jobs away from US-born workers, then we would expect the geographic areas of the USA with higher levels of recent immigration to have higher unemployment rates. A 2018 study by Dan Kosten,[3] however, found the following with regard to immigrants and unemployment in 2009: (a) counties in the USA with the lowest percentage of recent immigrants had an average unemployment rate of 4.6 percent; and (b) counties with the highest percentages of recent immigrants had an average unemployment rate of 3.1 percent.

This does not disprove the assertion that immigrants increase unemployment, but it is what we would expect to observe if they do not. It is possible that immigrants have been drawn to areas that have low unemployment, i.e., reverse causation. But if this were the case, then why do such regions continue to have low unemployment? The bottom line is that statistical results do not assure us of the direction of causation. We need, also, to 'taste the pudding'.

In 2019 we had more than 25 million immigrants in the US labor force, but the overall unemployment rate was at a 49-year low of 3.5 percent at that time. Clearly, 'the pudding' is inconsistent with the myth that immigrants and women take jobs away from Americans and men and, thereby, increase the overall unemployment rate.

4.2.3 Why Have Immigrants and Women Not Increased Unemployment Rates?

As pointed out in Chapter 2, traditional thinking has been that economic growth is essentially exogenous, i.e., it occurs independently of the state of the economy.[4] A growing economy needs more workers. Hence, immigrants, young people finishing school, and other new entrants into the labor market are usually absorbed with no increases in unemployment or decreases in wage rates. Even though there is merit to traditional thinking, it (in part) begs the question. That is, it says that new workers usually get jobs because the economy is usually growing. But why is it usually growing?

Many possible reasons for this exist, such as (a) advances in technology occur regularly; (b) the population and labor supply usually increase; and (c) successful firms almost always try to grow, thereby adding to the country's capital stock. In sum, it is reasonable to believe that economic growth occurs – at least in part – exogenously. However, this section suggests that increases in the labor supply along with general optimism can help to cause economic growth. That is, reverse causation can exist.

Conventional microeconomic theory about labor demand has no mechanism by which a firm will demand more workers if productivity, the product price, and the hourly nominal wage rate are constant. To explain, the standard theory is that a firm will hire progressively more units of labor as long as 'the revenue generated by the last unit of labor' is not less than the nominal wage rate. This extra revenue is called the marginal revenue product of labor (MRPL).

Traditional thinking seems to make sense, but it implies that (with productivity fixed) a firm will hire more units of labor only if the nominal wage rate decreases or the price of its product increases. According to this theory, there is no way that an actual or anticipated significant increase in the demand for a firm's product will (in itself) prompt it to hire more workers. Plain old common sense says that this has to be wrong! Firms will hire more workers if they anticipate a significant increase in the demand for their product, even if everything else is unchanged.

One problem with conventional thinking is that it assumes that firms are absolutely certain that they can sell the marginal product of the last unit of labor. However, in reality it often takes many months from the time that a product is produced (and labor and other costs are paid) until revenue is generated. Hence, firms are never sure about the magnitude of the MRPL, because there is uncertainty about market demand in the future.

The relevant measure of a worker's value to a firm is not the MRPL, but rather the 'expected value of the MRPL', E[MRPL]. This depends, in part, on the expected probability of selling the last unit of output at each possible price. The firm's perception of the future state of the economy will influence this subjective probability estimate.

The new idea here is that increases in the labor supply that occur when there is a general optimistic feeling about the economy can indirectly increase the demand for labor. How is this possible? Each firm knows that if it hires more workers, then any increase in the demand for its product(s) by the new employees is likely to be trivial.

However, if millions of firms are hiring more labor, then this can create an optimistic atmosphere with regard to future aggregate demand. The latter can increase the E[MRPL], and, hence, increase the demand for labor, with no increase in productivity, or product prices and no decrease in the wage rate. Increases in the labor supply can be absorbed without an overall increase in unemployment via the economic magic that optimism can generate.

In addition, optimistic expectations induce existing firms to expand, and new firms to arise. Such increases in the capital stock also generate an increase in the demand for labor. We need a rigorous theory of labor demand that takes account of the 'state of the economy', primarily via expectations with regard to future sales.[5]

It is important to understand the relevance of this digression into labor demand theory. As was just pointed out, traditional thinking assumes that new workers get jobs because economies usually grow, and firms need more workers. Furthermore, conventional thinking says that economic growth occurs primarily in an exogenous manner. However, no one has ever really explained why increases in the labor supply do not always cause more unemployment and/or lower wage rates.

Recall from Chapter 1 that it is relatively easy for people to accept a myth if no one really knows how and why a real-world event occurs. Consequently, we have the myth that jobs taken by immigrants or women take jobs away from American men. The position here is: Yes, economic growth occurs exogenously, but also increases in the labor supply along with optimism about the economy can help to cause economic growth. This reverse causation can legitimately be thought of as economic magic. It might very well be why, in general, overall unemployment does *not* increase with rapid increases in the labor supply.

4.3   TECHNOLOGY, COMPUTERS, AND ROBOTS

People have been predicting gloom and doom for workers from advances in technology for centuries. Of course, a dump truck or a computer can do the work of many people who transport dirt in wheel-barrels or do calculations by hand. There is no doubt that some people lose jobs directly when a significant advance in technology occurs. However, historically, advances in technology have (magically?) created more jobs elsewhere in the economy than are lost directly.

Someone must build and service the machines, computers, and/or robots that embody a new technology. Also, people will be working constantly to build better machines, computers, and robots. Furthermore, jobs will be created in the supply chain that provides the intermediate products and raw materials for the high-tech products. Then there will be jobs associated with the machine tools that are needed to install and maintain the high-tech equipment, and jobs involved in transporting everything. Finally, there will be more jobs in the financial and insurance sectors as a consequence of the increase in economic activity created by technological advances.

All of the above relate to upstream jobs (via Leontief's Law) generated by advances in technology that are embodied in new capital goods. Furthermore, each new job upstream creates more income and more spending (via Say's Law). This, in turn, leads to more jobs downstream (via Keynes' Law). As pointed out in Chapters 1 and 3, every new job upstream and downstream leads to another cause–effect chain of increases in production, incomes, spending and jobs.

One example of how an advance in technology creates more jobs than it destroys deals with Amazon, which processes packages with fewer workers; thus, some warehouse jobs are lost. This increase in efficiency allows Amazon to sell products more cheaply, thereby increasing its sales tremendously. The latter has led to the closing of perhaps hundreds of retail stores and losses of thousands of jobs, e.g. Sears, Toys R Us, and J. C. Penney.

On the other hand, Amazon has created hundreds of thousands of jobs. As of 2019 it had 798,000 people working for it globally, with more than 500,000 of these in the USA. The 500,000 does not include 900,000 jobs that Amazon says it supports in the more than 20,000 businesses that sell through Amazon.

In addition, advances in technology that require fewer workers to produce any one good, will free up labor to produce other products. For example, in 1850 roughly 50 percent of all workers in the USA were involved in agriculture. It took half of the labor force to produce enough food to feed everyone. Advances in technology gradually reduced the percentage of workers needed in agriculture. Farmers now represent less than 3 percent of the US labor force. Thus, agriculture's use of technology released millions of workers who could produce other products, thereby increasing GDP and the overall standard of living.

In sum, the 'test of the pudding is in the eating' principle strongly supports the idea that advances in technology typically have a large net positive effect on employment. This does not mean that no one is harmed, perhaps significantly. Nor does it imply that these losers should simply be written off as collateral damage.

4.4   INTERNATIONAL TRADE

Mythical statements (4) and (5) in Chapter 1 suggest that international trade is not good for a country, because imports decrease domestic employment. Allegedly, this is made worse if a country has excessive imports, i.e., a balance of trade deficit. In addition, Myth #7 claims that cheap foreign labor is one reason for the persistent US trade deficits. This section points out several facts that suggest that statements (4) and (5) are nonsense. Also, it briefly turns to the reason for deficits. Chapters 8 and 9 explore these topics much more thoroughly.

4.4.1   Economic Openness and Economic Growth Rates

First, turn to the idea that more international trade is, in general, not good for a country. Economists measure a country's 'economic openness' by adding the values of a country's exports (Ex) and imports (Im) and dividing this sum by the country's GDP.

  Economic Openness Index = [Exports + Imports]/GDP

There is a scholarly literature on how Economic Openness affects standards of living via economic growth rates.[6] Even though there is some disagreement, typically economic growth rates are positively correlated with Economic Openness, i.e., more open economies tend to grow faster.[7] This correlation is consistent with the hypothesis that more international trade causes faster economic growth. However, this correlation does not prove that more trade causes a country to grow faster. Maybe countries that grow faster decide that they want to be more open to international trade. Or perhaps there are forces that simultaneously generate faster growth and more international trade. We simply do not know!

4.4.2   Cheap Foreign Labor and US Trade Deficits

Next turn to the assertion that US trade deficits are caused in part by cheap foreign labor. Two facts are inconsistent with this. First, America does not import from only low wage countries. The USA buys much from Germany, especially motor vehicles such as BMWs, Mercedes, Volkswagens, Audis, and Porsches. Germany's labor costs are as much as 20 percent to 30 percent higher than in the USA. Indeed, BMW and Mercedes have built factories in the USA to take advantage of its relatively lower labor costs. The USA's most important source of imports is Canada, a country whose wage rates are not low. Another leading trading partner is Japan, where wage rates are relatively high.

The second fact is that the average wage rate in US exporting industries is about 20 percent higher than wage rates elsewhere in the economy. It is wage rates compared to labor productivity that matter, and the highly paid skilled workers in the export industries are very productive. A well-known study by Golub found that relative unit labor costs (wages compared to productivity) helped to explain trade patterns for the USA versus other countries.[8] Exports were positively correlated with lower unit labor costs that existed because productivity was proportionately higher than wage rates.

One scholar has found that, in general, union workers in the USA have obtained increases in their hourly wage rates at a faster rate than advances in their productivity. This has resulted in roughly 15 percent higher labor costs to union firms compared to nonunion firms.[9] Thus, many workers who have been harmed by cheap foreign labor might have unwittingly priced themselves out of a job.

4.4.3   Are Trade Deficits Associated with Higher Unemployment?

Next turn to the mistaken idea that trade balance deficits help to cause unemployment in the USA. Statistically this would imply that the trade balance (which is also called Net Exports) is negatively correlated with unemployment; that is, unemployment increases when net exports decrease, i.e., become more negative. Figure 4.1 shows US net exports from 1970 through 2019. The vertical shaded bars indicate economic recessions. Unemployment always increases during economic recessions (not shown).

Figure 4.1 indicates that net exports improved during the recessions of 1975, 1980, 1990, 2001 and 2008–2009, when unemployment was higher. Thus, unemployment went up when net exports went up – a positive correlation. The US economy experienced a cyclical upswing for 120 months during the 1990s. This caused the unemployment rate to trend downward in that decade. Figure 4.1 shows that net exports became progressively more negative (got worse) during the 1990s. Unemployment rates went down when net exports went down – again a positive correlation.

After the Great Recession ended in 2009, the economy had slightly more than ten years of a cyclical upswing with unemployment trending downward. But in Figure 4.1 net exports (with one exception) became more negative during this interval. Again, a positive correlation existed. The myth that a dete-

Source: US Bureau of Economic Analysis, Net Exports of Goods and Services [NETEXP], retrieved from FRED, Federal Reserve Bank of St. Louis; https://fred.stlouisfed.org/series/NETEXP.

Figure 4.1   *US net exports of goods and services 1970–2019*

rioration in the balance of trade is associated with higher unemployment is not only wrong, it has it precisely backwards!

4.5   HOW THE ECONOMY PERFORMED BEFORE THE CORONAVIRUS

An economy can be judged with regard to output and its growth rate, the average standard of living and how fast it improves, inflation, and unemployment. In addition, cyclical upswings and downswings (i.e., economic stability) are important.[10] From 1980 until 2019 US real GDP (the value of output using 2012 prices) increased approximately 180 percent; that is, it almost tripled from $6.8 trillion to $19.1 trillion.

In the 36 years from the end of World War Two until 1981 the economy had nine recessions. The upswings that followed the end of each recession had an average duration of less than four years. Then another recession would occur. In other words, people were cyclically laid-off rather frequently. However, in the 37 years from 1982 through 2019 there were only three cyclical downswings. In brief, the US economy has had far fewer recessions in recent decades.

After the Great Recession of 2007–2009 the economy experienced the longest cyclical upswing on record, more than ten years. However, the recovery from the Great Recession was initially slower than expected. This prompted some economists to fear that the 'good old days' of rapid economic growth were a thing of the past. The argument was, in part, that recent advances in technology do not boost output as much as they once did.[11] However, I strongly disagree with this position.

A deep recession causes thousands of firms to go out of business; workers drop out of the labor force; households and firms draw down their savings; and many people borrow excessively. It takes time for all of this to be reversed. Furthermore, our economy was on the brink of Great Depression #2 in 2007–2009. The fear (*black magic*) this generated took about four years to dissipate. Economic black magic in the form of negative economic hysteresis contributed greatly to the post Great Recession slow rate of growth.

Furthermore, I believe that the apparently smaller boost to output from recent innovations is less real than imagined because of measurement issues. Historically, many advances in technology have been associated with production techniques that increased productivity in the manufacturing sector. The resulting increase in the output of merchandise on assembly lines could easily be measured. Thus, GDP went up significantly in response to such advances in technology.

More recently, relatively more advances in technology have been associated with better hi-tech consumer products, e.g., flat screen HD TVs, super powerful personal computers, smart phones, and motor vehicles loaded with hi-tech features. There is no easy way to accurately measure how such technological advances contribute to GDP. For example, is a new iPhone equivalent to three bag-phones in the 1980s ... or five bag phones ... or maybe more? Consequently, the official data for GDP and its rate of growth are probably biased downward significantly.

A scholarly study by Byrne and Corrado calculates the effects of technological advances in IT services.[12] They consider the fact that the quantity of IT services used per person has increased significantly because of the much lower cost per unit of such services. Their conclusion is that this has increased consumer well-being each year by nearly $2,000 (2017 dollars) per connected user!

Also, they maintain that advances in IT technology along these lines increased actual US real GDP growth (compared to the official government statistics) by 0.6 percentage points per year over the 2009–2019 interval. This suggests that the USA's actual output in 2019 was about 6 percent ($1 trillion) higher than the official statistics – and this was just from measurement errors associated with IT services.

Another study on the contributions of advances in technology to well-being is that of Brynjolfsson et al. (2019). They point out that many free goods are not included in our measure of GDP. One of these is the services provided by Facebook. They conclude that from 2004–2017 the welfare gains from Facebook alone would have increased the US economic growth rate by up to 0.1 percent per year. Over this 14-year interval, the contribution from this one firm means that our true GDP would be almost 1.5 percent greater than the officially stated GDP; this exceeds $300 billion. All of this implies that the US economy performed significantly better than the decent marks it gets from official data.

Next, many people believe that the economy took off in the first three years of the Trump Administration, primarily because of tax cuts and deregulation. Table 4.1 shows that over the first three years of the Trump Administration the cumulative increase in real GDP was 7.3 percent and employment increased by 8.0 million jobs. However, in the last three years of the Obama Administration, the cumulative increase in real GDP was 7.0 percent, while employment increased by 8.3 million jobs.[13]

Table 4.1   *Obama versus Trump: the economy 2014–2019*

	Real GDP	Employment
Last three years for Obama*	+7.0%	+8.3 million
First three years for Trump**	+7.3%	+8.0 million

Notes:
* Time intervals: GDP = 2013:4 – 2016:4; Employment = January 2014–December 2016.
** Time intervals: GDP = 2017:1 – 2019:4; Employment = January 2017–December 2019.
Sources: FRED: US Bureau of Economic Analysis and US Bureau of Labor Statistics.

Chapter 11 documents that it took about four years for the economy to recover from the Great Recession. This represented an example of negative economic hysteresis. For the six years prior to COVID-19, the economy was doing OK … not great but OK! The decent performance during the last three years of the Obama Administration is especially noteworthy, because this occurred with higher corporate tax rates and many more government regulations. This is, indeed, perplexing!

Next turn to inflation and unemployment. The CPI inflation rate was very low in 1961, about 1 percent, and it gradually increased to 5.8 percent in 1970. The latter was high for an advanced economy. In the 1970s it initially declined and then escalated to 13.55 percent in 1980. Prices roughly doubled during the decade of the 1970s. The inflation rate came down in the early 1980s and stayed low, averaging around 2.5 percent for the 30 years before COVID-19. The high inflation that began in 2021 is addressed in Chapter 12.

The unemployment rate has been volatile, rising with each economic recession and falling during cyclical upswings. Unemployment trended upward during the 1970s, but has trended downward since 1981, primarily because of the two long cyclical upswings documented above. However, it shot up sharply in 2008 and 2009 in response to the financial collapse of 2007–2009 that almost took the US economy into Great Depression #2. It then became progressively lower until the end of 2019 when it hit a 49-year low of 3.5 percent.

4.6   THE USA VERSUS OTHER AFFLUENT COUNTRIES

All of the above data for the United States suggest that its economy performed reasonably well for many decades prior to the coronavirus. The pudding was good! But how has the USA done compared to other leading countries? Table 4.2 shows the cumulative percentage increase in real GDP over two time intervals for the USA and for six leading OECD countries (Canada, France, Germany, Italy, Japan, and the UK).

In the more recent interval the USA ranks first with a cumulative increase of 84 percent, while the mean for the other six countries is only 47.6 percent. Over the longer interval, the USA again ranks first with a cumulative increase in real GDP of 182.2 percent compared to a mean of 106.7 percent for the other countries. Clearly, the USA did great compared to other affluent OECD countries.

Table 4.2   *Cumulative increases in real GDP for leading OECD countries*

Country	Cumulative increase since 1980 (%)	Cumulative increase since 1994 (%)
Canada	+149.7	+81.6
France	+100.6	+50.4
Germany	+92.8	+41.0
Italy	+53.8	+18.3
Japan	NA	+26.0
UK	+136.8	+68.1
Mean of the above six	+106.7	+47.6
USA	+182.2	+84.0

Sources: FRED: OECD Real GDP Data, calculated from GDP indices, 2015 = 100.

Other measures of economic importance are the value for a country's average standard of living, and how fast this has been improving over time. The first column of Table 4.3 shows the average standard of living in 2019 for leading

Table 4.3   *Standard of living data: leading OECD countries, 2010*
                dollars

Country	Standard of living 2019	% change since 1980	% change since 1994
Canada	$51,589	75.7	51.2
France	$44,317	64.9	32.9
Germany	$47,628	82.2	38.6
Italy	$35,614	45.5	11.5
Japan	$49,188	90.2	24.7
UK	$43,688	99.8	45.6
Mean of above six	$45,337	76.4	34.1
USA	$55,670	94.7	47.2
EU	$37,104	88.2	47.2

Source: World Bank.

OECD countries. The USA is first with an average of $55,670 of output per person; the mean of the other six countries is $45,337.

Also, Table 4.3 indicates the cumulative percentage increase in each country's standard of living from 1980 until 2019 and from 1994 until 2019. In each interval the USA is a close second (behind Canada since 1994, and behind the UK since 1980). However, since 1980 the US average standard of living increased almost 95 percent compared to 88 percent in the EU, and 76 percent for the mean of the other six affluent OECD countries. Again, in spite of all the myths given in Chapter 1 and a myriad of difficulties, the US economy performed quite well compared to other leading countries over the 30 or more years before COVID-19.

NOTES

1. Source: Federal Reserve Economic Data.
2. See Budiman (2020), p. 1.
3. Kosten (2018).
4. Note that Paul Romer was awarded the 2018 Nobel Prize for his work dealing with the idea that devoting more resources toward education and R&D can make economic growth, at least in part, endogenous. See Romer (1994).
5. For an early first step along these lines see Balvers and Miller (1992).
6. A small sample of articles is: Dollar and Kray (2003); Edwards (1998); and Frankel and Romer (1999).
7. See Andersen and Babula (2009).
8. Golub (1995).
9. Hirsch (2008).
10. Many people believe that income distribution is also important. This topic will be addressed thoroughly in Chapter 7.

11. For an excellent scholarly discussion as to why US economic growth rates might be permanently lower see Gordon (2012).
12. Byrne and Corrado (2020).
13. Real Gross Private Domestic Investment (RGPDI) during the last three years of the Obama Administration (2014–2016) averaged about $3.1 trillion per year. The tax cuts and rapid depreciation laws passed by the Trump Administration appears to have stimulated RGPDI by about 10 percent to a mean of $3.3 trillion per year from 2017 through 2019.

5.   Advances in technology: magic and black magic

5.1   INTRODUCTION

When the coronavirus attacked us, it became the primary focus of most economic discourse. However, we will still have all of the economic issues that existed prior to the virus. One of these deals with the effect of rapid advances in technology on jobs, standards of living, and the distribution of income.

In recent years there have been a plethora of books and articles suggesting that we are now on the verge of developing computers and/or robots that will eventually displace a huge number of jobs, thereby possibly creating enormous problems for society. For example, one forecast is that robots might steal up to 800 million jobs by the year 2031.[1] Furthermore, it is possible that the pace of technological advances is too rapid for society to adjust properly.

Clearly, the incredible advances in technology over the last few centuries, and especially since the birth of the computer, have not caused massive unemployment. Indeed, just the opposite appears to be true (*economic magic*). However, there might still be cause for concern. The advances in technology in recent decades have created a wider gap between the haves and the have nots. Millions of people feel left behind, perhaps justifiably so. As the gap between winners and losers widens, political instability is likely to get progressively worse.

This chapter first considers traditional thinking about advances in technology and jobs, with ATMs as an example. Then it turns to the issue of the speed of advances in technology, and how 'too fast' is similar to the negative effects of Economic Darwinism at an extreme level. Next, Section 5.4 reviews the scholarly work on the polarization of the US workforce in recent decades.

Section 5.5 briefly discusses Moore's Law. After this, the chapter provides examples of resistance to advances in technology. This is followed by two examples of jobs that disappeared peacefully because of advances in technology, e.g., the Pony Express and lamplighters. The chapter ends with summaries of recent scholarly studies, the O-Ring Theory, and divergent opinions on the extent to which jobs will be eliminated via advances in technology.

5.2   TRADITIONAL THINKING ABOUT ADVANCES IN TECHNOLOGY AND JOBS

Scholars point out that machines in general, and robots and computers specifically, can be either complements with labor or substitutes for labor. Most of the existing reasons why so many jobs still exist after centuries of advances in technology use the complements versus substitutes ideas. These *microeconomic* ideas are logically correct, but they do not take account of the workings of the entire economy.

5.2.1   Computers and Workers are Complementary

Medical doctors use computers: (a) to search for cancer in X-rays and MRIs, and (b) to help them diagnose the health problem(s) of their patients. In addition, high-tech robots now perform surgeries, with a medical doctor supervising. Attorneys use computers to help them search for appropriate legal precedents. Auto mechanics use high-tech equipment to ascertain how well each piston in an engine is functioning. Economists often do econometric studies using hundreds of thousands of data points, and such activities would be impossible without modern computers.

5.2.2   Computers Substitute for Labor but Create Jobs

The Google Search software represents an advance in technology that is a combination of a substitute for some types of labor and is a complementary input for other types of labor. Google Search has virtually eliminated the need for traditional encyclopedias, e.g., Encyclopedia Britannica no longer has a printed version. This has decreased the demand for labor, paper and other inputs needed to produce and sell encyclopedia sets. However, as of March 2020 Google employed 102,000 full time workers, as well as 121,000 temps and contractors. This is trivial, however, compared to the 14.7 million workers that Microsoft directly employed globally way back in 2007.

It is very likely that the GPS technology has greatly reduced the demand for road maps, thereby decreasing the demand for workers needed to produce and distribute them. However, GPS makes it possible for firms such as Uber to exist. Uber CEO, Travis Kalanick, once maintained that Uber was creating 20,000 jobs per month.[2] Furthermore, such jobs can be high paying. For example, the *Washington Post* reported that in 2014 an Uber driver working 40 hours per week for one year earned an average of $90,766 in New York and $74,191 in San Francisco. In comparison, the average cab driver in New York earned about $30,000 per year.[3]

Similarly, the rapidly increasing service of delivering food to your home depends on GPS technology. It seems reasonable to believe that total employment in firms like Door Dash and Grubhub is in the tens of thousands. In 2011 it was estimated that downstream commercial GPS intensive industries in the USA generated 3.2 million jobs. Another 130,000 upstream jobs in GPS manufacturing industries existed. Finally, the number of jobs associated with the production of satellites needed for GPS and for the rockets used to put them into orbit is undoubtedly huge.

5.2.3   Other Explanations and an Example: ATMs

Sharpin and Mabry explain that if technology advances in the production of product A, then the price of A is likely to drop.[4] A lower price for product A will increase the quantity demanded for A which could increase the demand for labor to produce A. An example of this is ATM machines.

When Automatic Teller Machines (ATMs) were introduced in the 1970s many people thought they might greatly reduce bank teller jobs. The number of ATMs gradually increased in number to 100,000 by 1995. Then from 1995–2010 the number of ATMs in the USA grew to 400,000, only to increase to about 500,000 by 2019. ATMs are a cheap substitute for bank tellers, and, thus, they reduced the number of bank tellers per branch bank by one third. Consequently, the use of ATMs lowered the cost of operating a branch bank. As a result, many more branches were built, especially because many consumers choose the bank (and pharmacy) that is closest to their home.

No one knows the number of jobs that have been created upstream in the production of ATMs as well as in the construction of branch banks. Also, more jobs were created upstream in the industries that supply the inputs needed to produce ATMs and construct branch banks. All of these new jobs created more income, and, ultimately, increased the demand for the goods and services downstream, thereby creating even more jobs.

In addition, having more branch banks served to reduce the time (as well as the transportation and parking costs) associated with going to a bank. This increased the quantity of banking services demanded, which, in turn, stimulated the construction of even more branches.[5] The net effect of all this is that jobs for bank tellers did not decrease. Rather they increased by 50,000 from 1980–2010. This is a modest increase, but the point is that such jobs did not decrease!

5.3   THE SPEED OF ADVANCES IN TECHNOLOGY

The increase of technical efficiency has been taking place faster than we can deal with the problem of labour absorption.[6]

People are falling behind because technology is advancing so fast and our skills and
our organizations aren't keeping up.[7]

Most net positive changes in the world of economics create winners and
losers. Blacksmiths, carriage makers, and horse breeders suffered with the
development of the automobile. Thousands of family farmers had to give up
their farms because the cost of high-tech equipment made it very difficult for
a small farmer to survive. Similarly, in the 1950s 30 percent of the labor force
worked in the manufacturing sector. In 2011 this ratio was down to 10 percent.
Meanwhile, over this same time interval the percentage of workers in the
service sector increased from 50 percent to 70 percent.

If an economy slowly experiences advances in technology that eliminate
some jobs, this is similar to a country moving slowly toward globalization. The
slow movement means that the economy can more easily absorb those who
are displaced. It also makes it feasible for the government to have sufficient
resources to help those who feel left behind.

Alvin Toffler maintained decades ago that there are many reasons why
technology is advancing too fast.[8] Brookings Institution scholar Darrell West
suggests that robots, etc., make current advances in technology different from
those in the past.[9] He believes that the rapid advances in technology mean that
older positions will be eliminated faster than new jobs are created.

The significance of advances in technology that occur too rapidly is similar
to the fact that Economic Darwinism is good for an economy unless it occurs
too fast. Most economists strongly believe that efficient firms should expand
while inefficient firms should die off. Accepting this idea, however, does not
mean that there should be no limit to the speed with which inefficient firms
shut down.

The Federal Reserve and the FDIC encourage efficient banks to buy inefficient ones, but they sometimes allow a failing bank to close. For example,
from 1 October 2000 through mid-2018 there were 55 banks that failed in the
USA, and the Fed allowed 26 of these to close.[10] Contrastingly, during the
1929–1932 interval the Fed allowed roughly 4,000 banks to close. There can
be little doubt that this helped to cause the Great Depression.

Similarly, when Russia turned to its version of a market-oriented economy
in the early 1990s, it allowed inefficient firms to go under. Ostensibly, this was
a good idea. However, Russian managers had no experience with capitalism,
and government economic policies were suboptimal. Apparently, tens of
thousands of firms closed in the early 1990s. From 1992 until 1996 industrial
production in Russia decreased 50 percent.[11] In comparison, US industrial production fell by 47 percent during the first few years of the Great Depression.

In sum, Economic Darwinism is a good idea. However, too much of a good thing (like allowing too many inefficient banks and/or firms to close all at once) can be bad for an economy. Similarly, advances in technology that occur too rapidly can be a cause of economic black magic.[12]

5.4   POLARIZATION OF THE LABOR FORCE

It is well established that computers can easily replace middle skill workers whose tasks can be broken down into clearly defined steps, and therefore programmed into a computer. Hence, it is no surprise that many middle skill jobs have been eliminated via computers. Indeed, middle skill jobs made up 60 percent of all US employment in 1979, but only 46 percent in 2012.[13]

In general, there are two types of jobs that are difficult or impossible for today's computers to perform. The first type is highly skilled professional, technical, and managerial jobs that require much education and, more importantly, intuition and creativity. So far, computers and robots are not very good at intuition and creativity.

The second broad type is lower skill manual jobs such as food preparation, house and office cleaning, home health care, grounds maintenance, protection, and security. For example, house-cleaning workers never know exactly what type of mess they will run into, and where each mess will occur in a house, e.g., on a wall, in a toilet, inside the fridge, or on the couch. The appropriate action can vary greatly with each case.

Another example deals with home care for the elderly. The skill level needed is modest, but a home caregiver never knows exactly what is going to come up. Will the elderly person need meds, or a bath, or help getting dressed? In the last case, exactly what clothes will the older person want to wear today? If the older person is hungry then the choice of food and drink, as well as how the help is given can vary significantly.

David Autor and David Dorn have shed much light on the distribution of incomes and jobs in recent decades.[14] They have found that between 1980 and 2005 real wages increased for all skill levels, but they went up the most, more than 25 percent, for the most highly skilled workers. Workers with the least skill had their real wage rates rise by roughly 18 percent over the same interval. However, the middle skill workers had their wage rate increase the least, roughly 11 percent. The middle skill workers had their standards of living improve but feel left behind because others have gained more.

The second important finding by Autor and Dorn relates to how employment shares have varied with skill levels over the 1980–2005 interval. The middle skill workers had a decrease in their share of total employment.[15] The share of total employment for the highest skill workers went up almost 30 percent.

Surprisingly, the share of total employment for the lowest skilled workers went up as much as 24 percent.

If rapid advances in technology continue to squeeze out the middle class, it can lead to antagonistic, unstable, and dangerous politics. Clearly, this has been happening in the USA. Apparently, democracy does not work well if there are essentially two extreme points of view. Democracy requires compromises, and these appear to be more difficult without a large middle class.

5.5   MOORE'S LAW AND ADVANCES IN TECHNOLOGY

Advances in technology are occurring at a tremendous rate. Allegedly, there are currently more people engaged in research than the sum of all researchers who ever lived prior to now. In a study published in December 2017, the Euro Patent Office reported that patent applications in Europe had been growing by 54 percent a year.[16]

The distance between transistors on an integrated circuit is inversely proportional to the processing speed of a computer. In 1965, Gordon Moore noticed that advances in technology had doubled the number of transistors per square inch on integrated circuits every year. This has become known as Moore's Law. Current thinking has increased the time for doubling to 1.5 years, but the important point is that the speed of computing continues to double over and over within very brief time intervals.

When anything keeps doubling indefinitely, the long run consequences are too large to comprehend. For example, suppose that the maximum speed, and the miles per gallon, mpg, for a 1971 Volkswagen Beetle had been doubling every 1.5 years. Then by 2015 the Beetle would have had: max speed = 300,000 miles per hour, and mpg = 2 million![17]

A story
Allegedly, a long time ago a brilliant mathematician was in good favor with his king, who offered him any reward that he desired. The mathematician replied that his modest desire was to have one grain of rice placed on a square of a chess board. Then have two grains of rice placed on the next square; then four grains on the next square, etc. He wanted only the cumulative sum of grains on the entire chess board. Thus, his modest request was to receive the following number of grains:[18]

$$1 + 2 + 4 + 8 + 16 + 32 + 64 + 128 + 256 + 512 + 1024 + 2048 + 4096 + 8192 + \ldots$$
$$(2)^{63}$$

My smart phone tells me that $(2)^{63} = 9,223,372,036,854,775,808$. This is just the last magnitude in the equation, and the mathematician wanted the sum of this series. Supposedly, this amounted to all the rice ever grown in the country. Allegedly, so the story goes, the clever mathematician lost his head over this.

We have no idea what could lie ahead if Moore's Law continues to hold!

5.6   FEAR OF ADVANCES IN TECHNOLOGY

Marx predicted that the 'automatic system of machinery' would eventually replace all human workers.[19] Keynes referred to the Disease of Technological Unemployment.[20] Jeremy Rifkin asserted that high-tech is a deadly epidemic that destroys lives and destabilizes whole communities.[21] Perhaps the 1973 Nobel Prize winner, Wassily Leontief, best summarized the potential hazards of advances in technology.

> [T]the economy, and ultimately the society, must adapt to the conditions that technology creates.[22]

History records attempts to prevent industrial innovation as early as the sixteenth century. For example, in 1589 an English inventor named William Lee petitioned Queen Elizabeth I for a patent for his Stocking Frame Knitting Machine. He was turned down because the queen said it would make beggars out of her subjects. Later, Lee was turned down in France, and then again in England by King James I.[23] Eventually, however, an advanced version of Lee's invention helped the textile industry grow and prosper.[24]

However, on 11 March 1811, a group of English textile workers, the Luddites, destroyed factory equipment in Arnold, Nottingham. Such activities spread quickly throughout England over the next two years, eventually leading to bloody encounters between the Luddites and the British army. Eventually, Parliament made machine breaking a capital crime, and either executed or deported to Australia those who were found guilty.

5.7   JOBS THAT DISAPPEARED PEACEFULLY

An example of how an advance in technology destroyed jobs, but apparently did not cause social unrest, is the Pony Express. This relay of many horses and riders stretched 1,800 miles from St. Joseph, Missouri to Sacramento, California. Each rider traveled 75–100 miles at a time at high speed, changing horses every 10 to 15 miles. It allowed mail to be delivered in an average of ten days, which was in comparison to 25 days by stagecoach or several months by ships sailing around the tip of South America via the Strait of Magellan.

The company began delivering mail in April 1860, but abruptly halted service a few weeks later when the Paiute Indians waged the Pyramid Lake War. This temporary shutdown allegedly caused the Pony Express to lose $75,000, which was a whole lot of money at that time. Furthermore, the Pony Express died a quick death with the advent of the telegraph. It existed for only 18 months, from April 1860 until October 1861. Its failure displaced approximately 500 horses and 100 riders, including Buffalo Bill Cody.[25] This represents an excellent example of how an advance in technology can negatively affect some people, even a famous cowboy.

Another example of a job that was eliminated peacefully by technology was lamplighters, made popular by a song after World War Two. This song sentimentalized and memorialized the profession of lighting gas lamps at dusk, and then turning them off at dawn.[26] Gas streetlights started in Britain in 1792, and were first used for one street in Newport Rhode Island in 1803. Baltimore began using them more extensively in 1816, and their use grew progressively throughout the nineteenth century. The first electric streetlights in America were in Wabash, Indiana in 1880. Progressively more and more lamplighters lost their jobs as cities installed electrical streetlights, but it all happened peacefully.

5.8   MORE RECENT LITERATURE

A 2013 study by two Oxford University economists suggests that 47 percent of all jobs in the USA are at risk of being automated by the year 2033.[27] Also, MIT economist Daron Acemoglu and Pascual Restrepo of Boston University find that, from 1990–2007 in the USA, one more industrial robot per 1,000 workers reduced the labor/population ratio within commuting zones (local areas around a city) by 0.37 percent.[28] They conclude that this amounted to a loss of 6.2 jobs for every extra robot per thousand workers. Furthermore, it decreased wages by 0.73 percent.

Note that this study does not directly measure the effect of industrial robots on jobs. It shows only that the labor force participation rate is lower in areas where more robots are used. It is possible that such areas have many hi-tech firms that hire highly skilled and highly paid workers who have families with a smaller percentage of women who work outside the home. If so, then the so-called loss of jobs is deceptive.

Finally, as pointed out above, Darrell West suggests that robots, etc. really do make current advances in technology different from those in the past.[29] He believes that older positions will be eliminated faster than new jobs are created. This, he predicts, will lead to social unrest and political upheavals. It looks as though he was 'right on'!

5.9   O-RING THEORY

Chapter 7 documents that the rich and super rich have had their real incomes increase much more rapidly than everyone else. The exceptionally rapid increase for the richest 1 percent probably has many reasons for it. One is related to the rapid advances in technology and is called the O-Ring Theory.[30] If a chain has only one weak link, then replacing it is extremely important.

Computers and industrial robots can significantly increase efficiency and productivity for a firm. However, they cannot perform the duties of top management. If top management is bad then the cost to the firm is magnified, i.e., the large potential gain from efficient computers and robots is lost. In such a case, the computers and robots are equivalent to the many strong links in a chain, and the poor management is the weak link. Thus, it is very important to replace the weak link. This suggests that the value (and real wages) of highly competent managers have gone up substantially, at least in part, because of advances in technology.

A logical question is, 'OK, the O-Ring Theory helps to explain why top managers are paid so well, but what about the exorbitant salaries earned by athletes and entertainers? How do computers and robots increase their real wage rate?' The answer deals with advances in technology in general, rather than just computers and robots. Throughout most of recorded history an actor, singer, or musician could entertain only a few hundred people at a time in a theater or auditorium. In the early twentieth century an athlete could entertain only as many people as could crowd into a large stadium, perhaps up to 100,000.

Advances in technology allow actors to do their thing for tens of millions of movie goers, and perhaps an even larger number of people who buy the video version of their movie. Super Bowl games are viewed live by over 100 million and, supposedly, the World Cup Championship game has an audience of nearly one billion. In sum, advances in technology have very significantly increased the productivity of singers, actors, and athletes, thereby generating huge incomes for them.[31]

5.10   DIVERGENT OPINIONS

Harvard economist Kenneth S. Rogoff has said that it seems unlikely that millions of workers are headed to the glue factory like discarded horses. MIT economist David Autor has pointed out that, over the past two centuries, automation and technological progress have not made human labor obsolete. The US Patent Office says that IT intensive industries in the USA have 27.9 million jobs on pay-roles or under contract, and 17.6 million more jobs in their supply chain. The total of 45.5 million jobs represents almost 33 percent of all employment in the USA.[32] Furthermore, IT industries have very high wage rates. For example, the average salary for an engineer developing self-driving cars is more than $200,000. More generally, the IT sector has 47 percent higher wage rates than the average for all other sectors.[33]

There have been strongly divergent opinions about the effect that advances in technology will have on US jobs in the near future. In 2018 Erin Winick collected the predictions of 18 studies and summarized them in one table. The results are all over the map, ranging from a maximum loss of 80 million to a maximum gain of 13.6 million. Winick concludes by saying:

> There is really only one meaningful conclusion. We have no idea how many jobs will actually be lost to the march of technological progress.[34]

NOTES

1. Winick (2018), p. 1.
2. Eadicicco (2014).
3. Eadicicco (2014).
4. Sharpin and Mabry (1986).
5. Even though the Great Recession of 2007–2009 decreased their number, there were 80,000 branch banks in the USA in 2017.
6. Keynes (1932), p. 358.
7. Quote is from MIT professor Eryk Brynjolfsson as reported in Ross (2015), p. 40.
8. Toffler (1970).
9. West (2018).
10. One large investment bank, Lehman Brothers, was allowed to fail.
11. Smirnov (2015).
12. Slowing the pace of technological advances is not the same as stopping it or reversing it. See Tegmark (2017).
13. Kambayashi (2014).
14. Autor and Dorn (2013). Their results are summarized in a nontechnical manner by Rotman (2013).
15. A lower share of total employment does not necessarily imply that there were fewer jobs for that skill level.
16. Ghiselli (2018).
17. Yang (2018), p. 52.
18. A chess board has 64 squares.
19. Marx (1867).
20. Keynes (1932).
21. Rifkin (1995).
22. Leontief, as quoted in Caer (1996), p. 315.
23. Acemoglu and Robinson (2012).
24. Conniff (2011).

25.   The displacement of horses was more acute after the development of the automo-
      bile. In 1915 there were 26 million horses in the USA, but only 3 million in 1960.
      See Tegmark (2017), p. 126.
26.   The music was composed by Nat Simon and the lyrics written by Charles Tobias.
      It became a record in 1946 on the RCA Victor label, and spent 14 weeks on
      Billboard's Best Seller list, peaking at #1.
27.   Frey and Osborne (2013).
28.   Acemoglu and Restrepo (2017a). A nontechnical version of this is Acemoglu and
      Restrepo (2017b).
29.   West (2018).
30.   The 1986 explosion of the Challenger space shuttle was caused by the failure of
      a rubber O-ring seal in one of its booster rockets. It hardened and cracked from
      the surprisingly rare icy weather in Florida the night before. One weak link in
      a chain can be disastrous. See Kremer (1993).
31.   Rosen (1981).
32.   US Patent and Trademark Office (2016), as given in Hrdy (2017).
33.   US Patent and Trademark Office (2010).
34.   Winick (2018), pp. 3–4.

6.   Wage rates and jobs: myths and magic

6.1   INTRODUCTION

This chapter examines two of the economic myths given in Chapter 1. The first is that trickle-down theory (i.e., wage rates adjusted for price levels eventually increase with labor productivity) no longer holds. There are data that suggest that this is true. However, as pointed out in Chapter 1, the data are biased. Adjusting the data suggests that trickle-down is far from dead.

The second topic deals with the effect of higher wage rates on employment and unemployment. The myth is that higher wage rates always generate increases in unemployment, unless the higher wages are accompanied by proportionate advances in productivity. Presumably, this is especially true for increases in the minimum wage rate. There are many scholarly studies that support this, but the theories that underly them are microeconomic in nature. Hence, they might tell us nothing about the macroeconomic consequences of higher wage rates.

6.2   THE MYTH THAT TRICKLE-DOWN NO LONGER WORKS

6.2.1   Introduction

Thomas Sowell correctly pointed out that no one is credited with developing trickle-down theory.[1] The reason for this is probably because trickle-down simply follows logically from traditional microeconomic theory regarding labor demand. As pointed out in Chapter 4, this theory says that firms should hire progressively more labor provided that each new worker generates at least as much revenue per hour of work (when the firm sells that worker's marginal product) as the nominal wage rate. The extra revenue depends on the productivity of the workers as well as the selling price of the product. This implies that an advance in technology that increases labor productivity will generate an increase in the demand for labor.

Also, Chapter 4 pointed out that this theory implicitly assumes that firms are certain that they can sell all of the extra output that results from higher labor productivity. In the real world, this is typically not true. Thus, advances in labor productivity often lead initially to a decrease in labor demand. This means that initially, the benefits from an advance in productivity go primarily to the owners of the firms.

However, eventually firms will be able to sell all of the extra output (*economic magic?*). When this happens then labor demand increases, wage rates rise, and workers eventually (with a lag) benefit from advances in productivity. Casual empiricism and economic data allegedly suggest that trickle-down worked for many decades, but it has essentially stopped functioning over roughly the last 50 years.

6.2.2　Data That Imply That Trickle-Down is Dead

Phil Gramm and John Early point out that the average nominal wage rate (W = dollars per hour) in the USA went up from $3.99 in October 1972 to $23.26 in March of 2019, a 483 percent increase. However, prices (as measured by the consumer price index, CPI) also went up by 483 percent. Thus, these data tell us that the average real wage rate, W/CPI, did not change over this interval. This, in turn, implies that the typical wage-earning family was no better off in 2019 than they were roughly half a century earlier.[2]

Lawrence Mishel et al. reach essentially the same conclusion with slightly different numbers. They first show that labor productivity and hourly compensation (as measured by wage rates and benefits adjusted for inflation) moved very closely together from 1948 until the early 1970s. However, from 1973–2013 productivity was up 74.4 percent, but real hourly compensation increased only 9.2 percent.[3]

6.2.3　Tasting the Pudding Defies the Trickle-Down Data

Let's step back and taste the pudding by considering some of the 'stuff' that a typical family has now compared to 1970 or 1980. Here is a short list that is inconsistent with the myth that trickle-down has stopped functioning.

1.　Homes are bigger now and they are three times as likely to have central air conditioning.
2.　The percentage of households with a dishwasher is up roughly 70 percent.
3.　TVs are incredibly better … almost everyone has a color TV, and many families have a flat screen HD TV.
4.　Movie theaters now allow you to tilt your seat and stretch out; also, the theaters are stadium style so that you do not have to worry about sitting behind a very tall person or behind a woman with a big hat.

5. In the 1970s there were no cell phones; now we have smart phones, that embody, perhaps, the most advanced technology of any machine ever made.
6. Cars break down much less frequently, and they are more fuel efficient.
7. Only luxury cars had anti-lock brakes, power steering, air conditioning, and power windows then; now it is almost impossible to find a new car that does not have these.
8. Long distance telephone calls were extremely expensive then, as were airline tickets.
9. Most people did not have good/any health insurance.
10. Home computers did not exist 50 years ago. Now almost all families have one or more.

6.2.4   The Bias in Measuring Prices and Inflation

The official measures of the real wage rate, W/CPI,[4] are biased downward because the CPI has been biased upward for many decades. The CPI measures the prices every month of several hundred of the most frequently bought goods and services. The government determines how much people are buying of each good via a survey of thousands of households. Unfortunately, for many decades these surveys were taken very infrequently, i.e., many years apart. This generated an upward bias to official measures of inflation for several reasons.

First, people tend to buy a smaller quantity of products whose prices have been rising faster and buy more of products whose prices have been rising more slowly. But when the government calculated the CPI every month, it used the same quantities that were purchased when the last survey was taken, perhaps as long as a decade ago. Consequently, the CPI gave too much weight to products whose inflation rate had been high, and too little weight to products whose inflation rate had been low.

A second reason why infrequent surveys biased the CPI inflation rate upward deals with the fact that new high-tech products usually have high prices initially, and then their prices come down (sometimes rapidly) over time. However, cell phones were not included in the CPI until 1998, a full 14 years after they became available for consumers. Because they had not been included in the CPI, the index was not affected by the 75 percent drop in their prices over these 14 years.

A third reason for the bias in the CPI deals with improvements in quality. The government attempts to take account of improvements in quality. However, most economists believe that the official adjustments are not enough. For example, Byrne and Corrado of the Conference Board have calculated a broad price index for total mobile-phone service. They conclude that this price index declined 42 percent per year, whereas the Bureau of Labor Statistics had it declining only 4 percent annually.[5]

These biases mean that for many decades the officially stated rate of inflation for the CPI was biased upward about 1.1 percent each year. That is, the true inflation rate was about 1.1 percentage lower than the official government measure of inflation. Fortunately, for more than a decade now, the surveys are now taken much more frequently, and this bias has decreased. The official inflation rate for the CPI is now thought to be only about 0.6 percent higher each year than the true inflation rate. However, there still is an upward bias.

Seemingly small biases per year add up to a huge cumulative bias in the official data for the level of prices. For example, suppose for simplicity that the official yearly increase in the CPI had been 1 percent higher than the true inflation rate. Over a 30-year interval, this would mean that the official CPI would be about 33 percent higher than a true index of prices. Consequently, the incorrectly measured real wage rate, W/CPI, would be 33 percent lower than the true real wage rate. In such a case, it might seem as though trickle-down was not working, even if, in fact, it was operative.

6.2.5   Measuring the Real Wage Rate Correctly

Gramm and Early have come up with a measure of consumer prices that allegedly eliminates any bias.[6] When they calculate the real wage rate by dividing the nominal wage rate by their new (allegedly unbiased) price index, the results are startling! Their calculations suggest that the real wage rate has increased between 52 percent and 69 percent since 1972. They claim that labor productivity went up by 69.3 percent from 1979 to 2018. This suggests that real wage rates have essentially kept up with advances in productivity.

Objectively speaking the results depend on how one adjusts for the bias in the official CPI. Alternative methods for correcting the bias will give different results. However, it is certain that the upward bias in the CPI means that the assertion that the real wage rate has barely risen in recent decades is simply a myth. Defective economic data is an example of economic black magic, because such data can make people believe that the American economy has stopped functioning well. This can create a sense of pessimism (*black magic*), and a belief that capitalism needs to be radically altered or perhaps done away with.

6.3   WAGE RATES AND EMPLOYMENT

6.3.1   Microeconomic Theory

Many years ago Nobel Prize winner Milton Friedman emphatically stated that minimum wage laws create poverty.[7] As pointed out above, traditional microeconomic theory assumes that firms hire more workers as long as the revenue generated by each worker (from selling their hourly output) is not less than the nominal wage rate. If the wage rate goes up, then it will be profitable to hire less labor. This is logically sound, and it leads to the conclusion that a higher minimum wage will decrease employment, i.e., increase unemployment. However, this is a microeconomic perspective that does not consider the jobs that might be created via the extra spending of those who benefit from the higher minimum wage.

6.3.2   Empirical Evidence on Minimum Wage Rates and Employment

The Congressional Budget Office (CBO) has published a widely cited report – *The Effects on Employment and Family Income of Increasing the Federal Minimum Wage* – on the employment effects of alternative increases in the minimum wage rate.[8] They carefully considered the work of 11 different non-government published scholarly studies. Each of these implied a different response of jobs to increases in the minimum wage, with some finding that a higher minimum wage would actually *boost* employment.[9]

The 11 scholarly studies looked at the response of employment to increases in the minimum wage for specific types of labor (e.g., teenagers, or all low wage workers) or specific industries (e.g., restaurants) or geographic areas (cities or states). Each of the 11 studies used statistical procedures to come up with an 'employment elasticity'. The latter is defined as (the percentage change in jobs) divided by (the percentage change in the nominal wage rate, W). That is:

Employment Elasticity = (% change in jobs)/(% change in nominal wage rate)

If this is negative then a higher wage rate reduces employment, as in conventional thinking. The 11 scholarly studies used by the CBO Report had a median value for the employment elasticity of −0.25. The Report used the results of government population surveys to calculate how many workers would be affected directly by a higher minimum wage rate. Then they calculated the number of jobs lost via the equation:[10]

Jobs lost = −0.25 x (% change in W) x (Workers affected by higher min W)

The CBO Report says that 17 million workers would have their wage rates increase directly if the minimum wage went up to $15 per hour. But 1.3 million of these would lose their jobs. The 15.7 million who keep their jobs would have a total increase in their incomes that is much more than the loss in incomes for those who get laid-off. Thus, total labor income would go up significantly.

In addition, the CBO Report says that 'Another 10 million workers otherwise earning slightly more than $15 per hour might see their wages rise as well.'[11] The Report assumes that none of these 10 million would lose their jobs. Thus, total labor income would go up for two reasons, namely the higher wage rates for the 15.7 million directly affected and the 10 million indirectly affected.[12]

The CBO Report very carefully works through many details involved in how the increased income for those helped by a $15 minimum wage will affect the economy. For example, they consider that: (a) the cost of labor will go up, thereby decreasing business profit; (b) prices might rise because of higher labor costs; and (c) labor productivity might increase when workers are paid more.

They conclude that the higher minimum wage will have negligible macroeconomic effects on employment. The reason for this is that they assume that the economy will be close to its maximum sustainable GDP (i.e., potential output) by the time that the full effects of the $15 minimum wage work themselves out. All of this suggests that they *implicitly assume* that the higher minimum wage rate will not affect potential output and/or overall employment.

6.4   A MACROECONOMIC APPROACH TO HIGHER MINIMUM WAGE RATES AND EMPLOYMENT

The ideas in this section amount to heresy in the world of economics. Before proceeding, let us digress briefly on a medical finding that was initially considered to be absolute nonsense.

A story

For many decades doctors believed that stomach ulcers were caused only by excessive stress and too much gastric juices. Some patients had portions of their stomachs removed and some of them died. Then in the early 1980s an obscure Australian medical doctor, Barry Marshall, and his colleague, Robin Warren, discovered that almost all of their patients with stomach ulcers had a particular type of bacterium called Helicobacter pylori, or "H. pylori" for short. They also traced stomach cancer to this gut infection.

However, they could not cause ulcers by injecting H. pylori into lab mice. Thus, Marshall took some H. pylori from a patient, stirred it in a cup of broth, and drank it. In a few days he started to develop the symptoms of a stomach ulcer, which worsened rapidly. When he took an antibiotic, he was quickly cured.

He and Warren wrote up this result and sent it to a scholarly journal, which promptly rejected it, rating it in the bottom 10 percent of the papers they refereed that year. After much ridicule (everyone knew they were nuts) and effort, their work was eventually published and recognized. They shared the 2005 Nobel Prize in Medicine for a major discovery that was initially considered to be absolute heresy!

In a 2010 interview Marshall was asked if medical journals are still the gatekeepers of the status quo. His reply was: 'Now they might say, "It's so off the wall ... Is it true?"'[13]

6.4.1   Minimum Wage Rates and Economic Magic

This section suggests that a significantly higher minimum wage might conceivably generate a net increase in employment throughout the economy. Such an idea is similar to Barry Marshall's statement that the conventional wisdom about ulcers was wrong. That is, 'Everybody knows that higher minimum wage rates decrease employment. How could a Nobel Prize winner like Milton Friedman as well as most of the economics profession be wrong?'

The plan here is first to use some 'back of the envelope' calculations to obtain a rough estimate of the number of jobs that could be created via the extra spending by those who gain from a much higher minimum wage. Then we speculate about complications.

If an increase in the minimum wage to $15 directly affects slightly more than 15 million workers, then when the CBO Report was published the average wage rate of unskilled workers would have increased by at least $5 per hour.[14] A 40-hour work week comes to 2,080 work hours per year. Thus, the annual incomes of the directly affected workers will increase by $10,400. Multiplying this by 15 million workers means that a minimum wage rate of $15 would directly increase labor's income by roughly $156 billion.

The CBO Report does not consider how much the wage rate will rise indirectly for the 10 million workers whose current wage rate is $15 or slightly higher. Let's assume that this is $3 per hour, which amounts to a $6,240 annual increase in their income. Multiplying this by 10 million workers yields an increase in annual incomes of $62.4 billion for these workers.

With these assumptions, an increase in the minimum wage rate to $15 in 2019 would have increased total labor income by $156 billion + $62.4 billion = $218.4 billion.[15] Low-income households in the USA pay almost no income taxes, and they consume essentially all of their disposable income. Thus, aggregate demand for goods and services would rise, say, by roughly $200 billion.

An initial increase in aggregate demand of $200 billion by those who benefit from a $15 minimum wage would amount to roughly a 1 percent initial increase in overall aggregate demand, and as much as a 1 percent initial increase in output. If a 1 percent increase in output increases employment by 1 percent, roughly 1.5 million jobs would be created. This would more than wipe out the 1.3 million jobs that the CBO Report says will be lost directly.

Clearly, these numbers are not obtained in a rigorous manner. Hence, they might be way off, but they illustrate the point that the macroeconomic effects of a much higher minimum wage rate could conceivably be significant. Furthermore, these calculations relate only to the initial effects of a $15 minimum wage, and they omit many complications, some of which will now be reviewed briefly.

The CBO Report correctly points out that if firms do not raise their prices when higher wage rates increase production costs, then revenue and profits will go down.[16] Consequently, the incomes and spending of profit earners will decrease, but this will only partially offset the increase in spending by wage earners. Profit earning families will not decrease their spending (if at all) nearly as much as minimum wage families increase spending. Thus, the initial macroeconomic effect of the minimum wage hike will be a net increase in aggregate demand that initiates economic magic.[17]

The second complication deals with the economic magic that will follow the initial increase in aggregate demand. The well-known multiplier effect (via Say's Law and Keynes' Law) will increase incomes and spending over and over downstream. Also, upstream output, jobs, and incomes will occur via Leontief's Law. In sum, the complex nature of the economy serves to increase the number of jobs beyond any initial increase.

Next, consider the likely possibility that firms raise prices to cover any increase in labor costs from a $15 minimum wage rate. If they pass 100 percent of the $218.4 billion in higher labor costs along via price hikes, this would increase the nominal value of any given GDP by $218.4 billion. If nominal GDP had been $20 trillion, then it would rise a bit more than 1 percent to $20.22 trillion.

In other words, the $15 minimum wage rate would initially exert a one-shot permanent increase in prices by only about 1 percent![18] Furthermore, if output increases via the economic magic described above, then prices would rise by less than this. This would be the direct effect on prices – which seems small. However, if a $15 minimum wage and the ensuing 1 percent price hike created an 'inflation psychology' wherein all firms jumped at the chance to raise prices, then the outcome could be quite different.

The position taken here is not that a higher minimum wage rate is certain to have a net positive effect on employment. The economy is simply too complex for us to know what the net effect will be on employment from a much higher minimum wage rate. However, the loss in jobs directly from workers being laid-off when the minimum wage goes up, is certain to be at least partially (and perhaps significantly) offset by the macroeconomic effects of more spending.

6.4.2   Wage Rates and Employment During the Great Depression

The generally accepted idea that higher wage rates decrease employment applies to more than the minimum wage rate. It is commonly believed that any overall increase in wage rates for the entire economy will reduce employment, unless productivity goes up proportionately. Since this seems to make sense, and since our rigorous microeconomic theories confirm it, it seems like it must be true. Just like it must be true that stomach ulcers are not caused by a bacterium!

This section looks briefly at the relationship between nominal wage rates and employment during the Great Depression. We will see that the data are consistent with the hypothesis that economy wide changes in wage rates might conceivably affect employment in the same direction. That is, from a macroeconomic perspective, (up to a point) lower wage rates might reduce employment and higher wage rates might increase employment. This is just the opposite of conventional thinking. It is economic heresy!

The index of nominal wage rates decreased 22.6 percent from September 1929 until June 1933.[19] If higher wage rates decrease employment, then logically lower wage rates should increase employment. However, civilian employment decreased by 8.8 million over this interval.[20]

Chapter 10 explains that there are many reasons why employment decreased so much over this time interval. The point here is that a significant reduction in wage rates throughout the economy was associated with fewer jobs. This does not prove anything about causation, but it is consistent with the hypothesis that a general decrease in nominal wage rates will reduce aggregate demand, thereby causing a decrease in employment.

However, microeconomic theory tells us that the real wage, W/P, and not the nominal wage, W, is what matters for employment. From October 1929 until March 1933 the overall price index fell 32 percent,[21] and this exceeded the decrease in nominal wage rates of 22.6 percent. Thus, the real wage rate, W/P, increased between 1929 and 1933. This is generally given as one of the many reasons for the huge decrease in employment during the first few years of the Great Depression. This might be true, but it is based on microeconomic thinking ... not macroeconomic thinking!

The US economy started to recover from the Great Depression after 1932. Chapter 10 shows that by the end of 1936 real GDP had returned to approximately its 1929 value. The nominal wage rate increased by 38.7 percent from the middle of 1933 until 1937.[22] During this interval, total civilian employment increased by 7.5 million.[23] A higher nominal wage rate was accompanied by a substantial increase in jobs … not a decrease!

But wait a minute! Isn't it the real wage rate that matters? Maybe employment increased from 1933 to 1937, in part, because the real wage rate decreased? The overall price index increased 31.7 percent from March 1933 to June 1937.[24] The nominal wage rate was up 38.7 percent but prices increased only 31.7 percent. The real wage rate increased slightly from 1933 to 1937, but employment went up strongly. There could be many reasons for this. However, conventional thinking about how employment is affected by variations in the nominal wage rate uses the 'microeconomics real wage approach' to explain what happened to employment from 1929 through 1932. From 1933–1937 the 'microeconomics real wage approach' is inconsistent with what happened.

What is the point of all this? It is related to the idea that an increase in the minimum wage rate could conceivably increase the number of jobs in the economy. If this were true, then perhaps: (a) lower nominal wage rates at the beginning of the Great Depression helped to decrease employment; and (b) higher nominal wage rates from 1933 to 1937 helped to create jobs. In the words of a famous Nobel Prize winning doctor: 'It's so off the wall … is it true?'

6.5   POSTSCRIPT

Please understand that I am not suggesting that continuous rapid increases in nominal wage rates are the key to super-prosperity. That would be nonsense! Continuous rapid increases in nominal wage rates would require the nominal money supply to grow rapidly, thereby generating a high inflation rate, which could severely harm the economy. The objective here is to make it clear that conventional thinking about nominal wage rates and jobs is a microeconomic idea, that might be highly misleading (or totally wrong) with respect to the overall macroeconomic effects of higher wage rates.

NOTES

1.   Sowell (2019), p. 137.
2.   Gramm and Early (2019a), p. A15.
3.   Mishel, Gould and Bivens (2015), p. 4.
4.   W denotes the nominal wage rates in dollars per hour, and CPI represents the Consumer Price Index.
5.   Byrne and Corrado (2020).

6. Gramm and Early (2019a).
7. Friedman (1962).
8. Congressional Budget Office (2019).
9. Ibid., p. 27.
10. They did this calculation several times by assuming different percentage increases in the nominal wage rate, W.
11. Congressional Budget Office (2019).
12. The CBO Report, p. 28 says: 'there is evidence of publication bias in the minimum-wage literature, suggesting that the published elasticities might systematically overstate the true elasticity.' On the issue of publication bias see: Card and Krueger (1995) and Andrews and Kasy (2017).
13. Weintraub (2010).
14. This conservatively assumes that the mean hourly wage for unskilled workers in 2019 was $10 per hour.
15. This example omits the loss of income for those who get laid-off. However, this could be relatively small because of unemployment compensation benefits and welfare payments. The calculations here also omit other real world complexities.
16. Congressional Budget Office (2019), p. 33. Note that two scholarly studies find that firms absorbed essentially all of any increases in labor costs when the UK introduced a national minimum wage in 1999. See Draca, Machin and Van Reenen (2011) and Bell and Machin (2018).
17. The CBO Report, p. 34, acknowledges this by saying: 'Because they [higher minimum wage rates] would transfer income toward families with lower incomes, the options [different amounts of an increase in the minimum wage] would increase overall demand and family income in the first few years after they were initially implemented.'
18. This 1 percent increase in prices via a macroeconomic approach is slightly less than what scholars have found via a microeconomic approach. For example, Renkin, Montialoux and Siegenthaler (2022) find that a 10 percent increase in the minimum wage increases prices by about .36 percent in supermarkets. Also, Leung (2021) concludes that a 10 percent increase in the minimum wage increases overall retail prices by .24 percent to .32 percent. If the nominal wage rate goes from $10 to $15 this 50 percent increase would imply higher grocery store prices of 1.8 percent in Renkin et al., and higher overall retail prices of about .96 percent to 1.6 percent in Leung.
19. The index went from 104.4 to 80.7 over this time interval.
20. Employment went from 47.6 million to 38.8 million over this interval.
21. The price index fell from 181 to 123.
22. The wage index went from 80.7 in June of 1933 to 111.9 in December of 1936.
23. Jobs went from 38.8 million to 46.3 million over this interval.
24. The price index went from 123 to 162.

7. Poverty and income inequality: myths and magic

7.1   INTRODUCTION

As pointed out previously, in my opinion, one bad aspect of the US economy deals with poverty and the unequal distribution of income. Although the latter might or might not affect a country's economic performance (more on this below), it can lead to political turmoil and even violence. Furthermore, poor people are typically those who have not obtained many productive skills. If this is caused by an inefficient education system, then society has not utilized the potential inherent in its population. Finally, society must decide how much we want to help those who are poor, simply because it is the right thing to do.

It is important to understand the difference between poverty and income inequality. The definition of poor or poverty is, like all definitions, arbitrary, and can be debated with respect to its relevance. However, income inequality is tied up with facts that (theoretically) cannot be debated. The percentage of all income earned by the poorest 20 percent versus the income earned by the richest 20 percent are data, plain and simple. Unfortunately, scholars have disagreed about how we measure these facts.

Research in recent years has shown that it is not simply the actual level of a person's income that matters to them, but rather their perception of where they are in the economic ladder of success.[1] For example, the poorest 20 percent in America have a higher standard of living (on average) than they did 30 or 40 years ago. However, many of them feel worse off. The same is true for the middle 20 percent of all income earners (somewhere around $40,000 per year). They feel left behind even though their standard of living has also improved. These perceptions exist because the gains to the poor and the middle class have been minuscule compared to the gains to the affluent, the rich, and the super-rich.

There are facts that suggest that poverty and/or income inequality create health and social problems. For example, Wilkinson and Pickett constructed an index of ten factors that affect health and social problems for many affluent countries. This index was very positively correlated with income inequality, i.e., greater inequality was associated with more health and social problems.

This was also true for the 50 states in the USA.[2] Of course, correlation does not prove causation.

Before proceeding, let me state my feelings and thoughts about this issue. First, I do not completely believe the results of any one published work on poverty and income inequality, because many studies come up with very different conclusions. I believe that no one cheats. However, some highly respected scholarly works measure poverty and income inequality in a particular way, and conclude that things look terrible. On the other hand, measuring poverty and income inequality in other seemingly reasonable ways suggests that things are not nearly as bad.

Politicians and lobby groups can always find scholarly evidence to support their agenda. Liberals say that the US version of market capitalism has failed miserably by leaving tens of millions of people behind, and that we should radically restructure our economy and move toward a welfare state, or, more dramatically, toward democratic socialism.

At the other extreme, conservatives say that we need income inequality to provide incentives. The strong incentives that have been provided by our unequal distribution of income have created an economic giant, and 'a rising tide lifts all boats'. I strongly accept this statement, but what if some boats are 90 ft luxury yachts, and many others are little row boats with leaks?

Conservatives maintain that a more equal distribution of income will kill economic growth. If so, then eventually everybody (including the poor) will be worse off. This chapter maintains that such an assertion is simply a myth; scholarly evidence does not, in general, support this point of view. In addition, as pointed out above, the economic performance of the Nordic countries has been better than the experiences of other affluent countries who have much greater income inequality.

7.2   THE OPTIMUM COMBINATION OF RICH VERSUS POOR

People who are struggling will tend to say the level of inequality is excessive, but those who have benefited from the current system will state that it seems to be working just fine.[3]

I wonder if it is necessary for people to earn and take home tens of millions of dollars per year in order for them to work extremely hard in any profession. Equivalently, is it necessary for successful entrepreneurs to earn billions of dollars in order for them to accept the risk associated with business? We absolutely need incentives! Highly productive people should be rewarded compared to less productive people! But how much is needed to provide the proper incentives.

This is not to say that super high-income people should not have the fruits of their often lifetime of hard work and risk taking. Rather, I am questioning the argument that they need the rewards that now exist in order to motivate them properly.[4] For example, does anyone think that Willy Mays or Hank Aaron would have performed better if they had been paid the equivalent of the enormous salaries now earned by super-star athletes? The critical question is: 'Is there an optimum degree of inequality?'

Let's digress for a moment on the idea of trade-offs. In the 1970s when gasoline prices sky-rocketed, speed limits on interstate highways were lowered to 55 mph, because driving more slowly saves gasoline. We discovered that driving more slowly also saves lives. This prompted some people to argue that we should keep the 55 mph permanently.

The logical reply to this argument was: 'If 55 mph on interstate highways saves lives, then maybe the speed limit should come down to 45 mph ... or perhaps 35 mph. Even more lives will be saved!' The truth is that there is a trade-off between speed limits and fatal accidents. Society must decide what it considers to be the optimum combination of the two.

As another example, some people have said that the best way to provide more medical services for the poor would be to have many more doctors. This, however, would require medical schools to expand. Critics of this idea say that if we expand all med schools, then people will be admitted who are not deemed good enough to get into a med school now. Thus, the quality of new doctors would go down.

For the sake of argument, assume that expanding all med schools would reduce the quality of medical care significantly. This, of course, need not be true; it might reduce the quality trivially, if at all. If so, then *contracting* the size of all med schools would increase the quality of medical care. Thus, maybe every year we should admit only the top two or three applicants into each program. Just think how much better the average new doctor would be.

The point is obvious. As with speed limits, we have a trade-off situation, and society should decide on the optimum number of new doctors, just as it has to decide on the optimum speed limit. This also applies to financial incentives via an unequal distribution of income. Logically, there has to be an optimum degree (or maybe an optimum range) for income inequality. It is unrealistic to blindly believe that we have this now.

7.3   PEN'S PARADE

In 1971, the Dutch economist Jan Pen came up with a clever idea to illustrate the uneven distribution of income in England.[5] At that time, income inequality in the USA was greater than in England. Since then, income inequality has increased in both countries. Pen asked you to pretend that you are watching a parade of everyone in the country, with each person's height proportional to their income. In this situation, your height equals the average (mean) height in the country. Everybody marches past you in just one hour, with the shortest (poorest) people first.

In the first few minutes the people are tiny, with some so small that you can barely see them. These are primarily people without regular work. Full time workers start to march past after ten minutes. Most of them are barely waist high to you. These are unskilled manual workers, unskilled clerical workers, burger flippers, etc. After 30 minutes, people with the median income walk by; they are not quite 5 feet tall. According to Pen, these include experienced tradesmen, many craftsmen, skilled office workers, school teachers, and some unskilled factory workers.

After about 45 minutes you see people walking by who are as tall as you, i.e., they have the mean income. Note well that it takes 45 of the 60 minutes to get to this income. This means that 75 percent of the people have less than the average (mean) income, because the mean is biased upward by the rich and super-rich.

After 54 minutes the richest 10 percent of the population start to go by. The first of these are about 20 feet tall. They include family doctors, the average attorney, highly paid professors, top civil servants, and some very successful small business owners. After 59 minutes you see people like corporate executives, highly specialized medical doctors, many professional athletes, top stockbrokers and investment bankers, etc. They are 50 feet, 100 feet, and even 500 feet tall.

In the final few seconds of the one-hour parade, giants march past you. These super-rich people include pop stars, movie stars, super models, super star athletes, CEOs, and top entrepreneurs. Their height is measured in miles, with their heads disappearing into the clouds. Indeed, the richest ones have the heels of their shoes more than 100 feet high.

A comment

The rest of this chapter contains tables and charts that include a plethora of numbers associated with the distribution of income. I have difficulty obtaining a proper perspective between annual incomes of $10,000, $50,000, $1 million, and $50 million. For me, Pen's parade helps to bring these numbers to life, because I can visualize the difference between people who are: a few inches tall; five feet tall; 100 feet tall; and up-in-the-clouds tall.

7.4   POVERTY IN THE USA

7.4.1   Official Government Measures

Government statistics imply that (with one exception) there has been very little progress in reducing poverty in the USA over the last four or five decades. Table 7.1 shows the data on the percentage of the USA population that are officially poor. The poverty rate for people 65 and older fell significantly from 29.5 percent in 1966 to 9.7 percent in 2018. The poverty rate for children (those less than 18 years of age) was 17.6 percent in 1966 and has been roughly the same in recent years.[6] Similarly, the poverty rate for non-senior adults (ages 18 to 64) has been roughly unchanged since 1966.

Table 7.1   USA percentage in poverty 1966–2018

Year	Less than 18 years	18–64 years	65 years+
1966	17.6	10.0	29.5
1976	16.0	8.8	14.1
1986	20.5	10.6	12.5
1996	20.5	10.9	10.5
2006	17.4	10.9	9.7
2016	18.0	11.6	9.3
2018	16.2	10.7	9.7

Source: FRED: US Bureau of the Census, Current Population Survey.

As pointed out above, the method used by the government to measure poverty is flawed. In 1955 the government took a survey of total expenditure by households of different sizes. This included expenditure by each household on enough food for good nutrition. They found that the cost of food was approximately one third of their annual spending.

In the early 1960s the government decided to use the results of this survey, and it defined the 'poverty threshold income' as three times the dollar cost of food. For example, in 1959 this food cost was about $489 per year for one person. Thus, the poverty threshold for a single person in 1959 was 3 × $489 = $1,467 per year, as shown in Table 7.2. Any person with less income would be called poor. Naturally, the poverty threshold goes up with the size of a family, as is shown in Table 7.2, which has poverty thresholds for one, two, and four people.

The government increases the poverty threshold every year by the inflation rate in the Consumer Price Index, CPI. Table 7.2 indicates that the poverty threshold for one person increased 8.7-fold from ($1,467 in 1959) to ($12,784 in 2018). This implies that the official CPI in 2018 was 8.7 times as high as it was in 1959. However, we know from Chapter 6 that the official CPI inflation rate has been biased upward for many decades.

Table 7.2   USA poverty threshold incomes 1959–2018

Year	One person ($)	Two people ($)	Four people ($)
1959	1,467	1,894	2,973
1970	1,954	2,525	3,968
1980	4,190	5,363	8,414
1990	6,652	8,509	13,359
2000	8,791	11,235	17,604
2010	11,137	14,216	22,315
2018	12,784	16,247	25,705

Source: FRED: US Census Bureau, Current Population Survey.

This affects the poverty threshold incomes, and, hence, the percentage of people who are officially poor. Meyer and Sullivan maintain that correcting for the CPI bias means that the overall poverty rate between 1980 and 2010 fell 2 percent, as opposed to rising 2 percent via the official data.[7]

Even though correcting for the upward bias in the CPI reduces the over official poverty rate, as pointed out in Chapter 1, multiplying the cost of food by three to obtain the poverty threshold income is very unrealistic. To repeat for emphasis what was said in Chapter 1, Table 7.2 indicates that the income threshold for a single person to be officially poor in 2018 was $12,784 per year. This implies that a single person earning more, say $12,800 per year, would not be officially classified as poor. $12,800 per year is about $6.15 per hour for a 40-hour work-week. By any reasonable standard, working for $6.15 per hour would make a person 'damn' poor!

People might have spent 33 percent of their income on food in the 1950s, but now it is closer to 15 percent or 20 percent, depending on their income level.[8] Consequently, the poverty threshold income should be about five or six times the cost of food, thereby greatly increasing the dollar value for the poverty threshold income.

For example, if the average poor person spends 20 percent of their income on food, then we must multiply the cost of food by five instead of three to obtain the poverty threshold income. For one person this would mean that in 2018 a single person was poor if they earned less than $21,307 per year, not $12,784 as in Table 7.2.[9] This would significantly increase the official number of poor people in the USA! Right now, by using any reasonable standard, we have no idea how many people are actually poor!

7.4.2   Alternative Measures of Poverty

When measuring the extent of poverty, the government does not obtain data from income tax returns. Rather the Bureau of the Census gets income data from the Current Population Survey. No attempt is made to determine the accuracy of what each family reports as their income. It takes them at their word.

Bruce D. Meyer and James X. Sullivan are highly respected experts on the measurement of poverty rates.[10] They find that in 2010 only 36 percent of food stamp money was reported. Another 20 percent was imputed by the government. This leaves 44 percent of total food stamp money omitted from government calculations of income.[11]

In addition, a Consumer Expenditure Survey by the government is used to calculate how much each family spends on consumer goods. Meyer and Sullivan have compared the reported (from these surveys) total consumption of the poor with the reported total incomes of the same group. The results are spectacular! Reported expenditures for the poorest 5 percent were seven times greater than their reported incomes.[12]

Meyer and Sullivan have calculated poverty rates using consumption-based measures of income, and using unbiased inflation data. They found that from 1960–2010 the overall poverty rate in America decreased by 26 percent. In sum, they correctly conclude that there is a smaller percentage of the population who are officially poor if we: (a) calculate the poverty threshold by adjusting for the bias in the CPI; (b) calculate total expenditure on consumption as a proxy for incomes; and (c) compare (a) with (b).

However, if they used the government's calculation method for obtaining the poverty threshold income (i.e., 3 × $cost of food), they tell us nothing about how many people are actually poor by reasonable standards. In sum, we very likely have made progress on reducing poverty, but no one knows the true extent of poverty.

7.5   INCOME DISTRIBUTION IN THE USA

Emmanual Saez and Thomas Piketty have published many influential scholarly papers on income distribution in the USA.[13] One of their findings is that the share of pretax income in the USA earned by the top 10 percent: (a) varied between 45 percent and 48 percent from 1917 until the late 1930s; (b) dropped sharply to about 35 percent by the end of World War Two; (c) stayed near 35 percent until the late 1970s; and (d) has been rising steadily for about the last 50 years, hitting 48 percent in 2016. At that time the richest 10 percent earned almost as much as the total incomes of the poorest 90 percent.[14]

Their work has had significant consequences. It earned Saez the John Bates Clark Medal, the top award for an academic economist in the USA. Also, it helped make Piketty's book, *Capital in the 21st Century* an international best-seller. Furthermore, their work has provided strong scholarly evidence for people who favor policies to redistribute income more evenly. Indeed, Peter Orszag, President Obama's budget director, reportedly said that Saez's work had a significant impact on Obama's budget.[15]

There is controversy with regard to this study. Their data came primarily from income tax returns. Unfortunately, prior to 1939, state and local government employees were not mandated to file tax returns. Also, in many years before 1940 only about 10 percent of all people in the USA filed tax returns, because their incomes were too low to require this.[16] Thus, the very high percentage earned by the rich prior to World War Two is really just an educated guess. Furthermore, the incomes used in the study do not consider the taxes paid by the rich or the government transfer payments (welfare) to the poor.

Saez and Piketty maintain that the rapid decrease in inequality which took place during the Great Depression was a result of Congress and Roosevelt increasing the top marginal income tax rate to 91 percent during the New Deal and World War Two. This has been used recently by political progressives who argue for much higher taxes for the wealthy.

Geloso et al. say that Piketty and Saez's (P&S) results are biased because of measurement errors.[17] More specifically, they conclude that P&S overstate the very high degree of inequality before 1929. Thus, the rapid decrease in inequality during the Great Depression and World War Two is also overstated. Furthermore, Geloso et al. suggest that the decrease in inequality over this time interval was not caused primarily via the high marginal tax rates, but rather by the huge decrease in stock and other asset prices.

Also, Piketty et al. found that the richest 1 percent's share of national income, after taking account of taxes, increased from 9 percent in 1979 to 20.3 percent in 2014.[18] Two federal government economists, Gerald Auten (Joint Committee on Taxation) and David Splinter (US Treasury Department, Office of Tax Analysis) redid the Piketty, Saez, and Zucman study. They found that the top 1 percent's share of after-tax income increased much less, i.e., from 8.4 percent in 1979 to only 10.1 percent in 2015.[19] This huge difference created a controversy.

Why did they get such different results? The most important reason is that Auten and Splinter took account of government transfer payments. The poor receive much more in government transfer payments than they pay in taxes. On the other hand, the rich pay a huge amount of taxes and receive essentially no direct government transfer payments. Other reasons for the different results deal with alternate procedures and assumptions that were made when working with the data. The two sides have gone back and forth in a scholarly debate, and the details are too involved to be included here.

Comment

One side says that increases in the USA's average standard of living in recent decades have benefited the rich unbelievably more than the poor. The other side says that the rich have gained more than the poor, but not exceedingly so. Whom do we believe? Perhaps it does not matter. All studies agree that the gap between the rich and the poor has been increasing steadily. The relevant questions should be: (a) is the increase in income inequality desirable?; and (b) is it sustainable?

If the answer to (a) and (b) is 'no', then is there a better way to 'fix it' than simply levying higher taxes on the rich and transferring the funds to the poor? Christopher Leonard argues convincingly that the easy money policy of the Fed ever since the Great Recession has greatly inflated stock and bond prices, and, hence, contributed to the wider gap between the rich and everyone else.[20] His position on this topic is very convincing.

7.6   INCOME INEQUALITY IN THE USA VERSUS OTHER COUNTRIES

A measure of income equality that is commonly used is a Gini coefficient, or just 'Gini' for short. Table 7.3 gives the Gini coefficient for seven countries in 2018.[21] The data imply that income is distributed more unevenly in the USA than in any of the other countries. The mean Gini for the other six countries is .314. However, Gramm and Early maintain that these Gini calculations do not compare apples with apples; that is, these Ginis use incomes that are measured differently in the USA than in other countries.[22] More specifically, the US Gini omits several government transfer payments that are included by other countries. These include: $760 billion of Medicare and Medicaid payment to the poorest 40 percent in the USA; $520 billion from 93 other Federal transfer programs; and $310 billion in transfer payments by state and local governments.

Table 7.3   Gini coefficients for seven affluent countries 2018

USA	UK	Australia	Japan	Canada	France	Germany
.39	.34	.33	.32	.31	.295	.29

Source: OECD.

When these transfer payments are taken into account, then the Gini for the USA comes out to be .32, which is minutely higher than the mean Gini for the other six countries. This much more favorable Gini coefficient for the USA arises because the poorest 20 percent in America obtain much of their disposable income from government transfer payments. In sum, according to Gramm and Early, America's distribution of income does not differ significantly from other large affluent countries.

Note, however, that Gramm and Early add Medicare and Medicaid payments to the incomes of the poor, but they do not add employers' contributions to pensions and health insurance to the incomes of (primarily) the non-poor. The Gini for the USA would increase if these contributions were included, because they were close to $1.5 trillion in 2019.

7.7   INCOME INEQUALITY AND ECONOMIC GROWTH

As pointed out above, a standard argument against income redistribution is that it kills incentives and reduces economic growth rates. Allegedly, the poor might eventually be worse off after many years, because they will be getting a larger portion of a GDP pie that is not as big as it would have been without redistribution. This section looks at evidence related to conventional thinking in two ways. First we compare the rate of increase in real GDP for the Nordic countries (where income inequality is relatively low) with economic growth in the USA and other countries. Then we summarize the results of scholarly studies on this topic.

7.7.1   Economic Growth Rates in the Five Nordic Countries

Table 7.4 shows cumulative percentage increases in real GDP for 10 countries for the 27 years from 1993 to 2020. The cumulative growth for the non-Nordic countries ranges from a low of 31 percent for Japan to a high of 93 percent for the USA. The mean for these countries was a cumulative increase in output of 63.5 percent.

Table 7.4   Cumulative OECD economic growth 1993–2020

Five non-Nordic countries		Five Nordic countries	
USA	93%	Norway	82%
UK	73%	Denmark	57%
Germany	51%	Finland	80%
Japan	31%	Sweden	97%
France	45%	Iceland	120%
Mean	63.5%	Mean	87.2%

Source: FRED. The interval was from 1990–2017 for Germany and Denmark, and from 1995–2020 for Iceland.

The cumulative growth over the same time interval for the five Nordic countries ranges from 57 percent for Denmark to 120 percent for Iceland. The mean for these five countries was a cumulative increase in output of 87.2 percent. Recall the discussion surrounding Table 7.3 that the mean Gini for the six countries in that table (excluding the USA) was .314. The mean Gini for the five Nordic countries is .266.[23] Income is distributed much more evenly there, but they have grown more rapidly. Of course, this proves nothing about causation. There could be many reasons why these relatively smaller countries have grown more rapidly. The point is that they have a much more equal distribution of income and they have not grown slowly.

7.7.2 Scholarly Studies on Income Distribution and Economic Growth

> The problem is that ... the net [theoretical] effects of inequality on investment and growth are ambiguous.[24]

Traditional thinking (that less inequality reduces economic growth rates) seems to make sense, but as the above quote says, scholarly theoretical work indicates that income inequality can affect economic growth in many different ways, with the net effect uncertain. Statistical studies are consistent with this theoretical conclusion. Here is a small sample.

1. Persson and Tabellini and Alesina and Rodrik find that economic growth rates go down when income inequality increases.[25] This is the opposite of traditional thinking.
2. Li and Zou and Forbes find that economic growth rates increase when income inequality increases.[26] This is the traditional point of view.
3. Barro concludes that:[27] (a) higher inequality raises growth rates in advanced economies; (b) higher inequality reduces growth rates in developing economies.
4. Banerjee and Duflo find that the rate of economic growth goes down any time that the degree of income inequality changes.[28]

Comment
An objective observer has to conclude that we simply do not know how income inequality affects economic growth rates. If so, then those who argue against a more equal distribution of income because it will reduce economic growth are unwittingly promulgating a myth!

NOTES

1. See Payne (2017).
2. Wilkinson and Pickett (2010).

3. Payne (2017), pp. 24–25.
4. One could argue that the rich and super-rich are entitled to the fruits of their labor simply because this is fair.
5. Pen (1971). See also Crook (2006).
6. Allegedly, the stimulus checks because of the coronavirus pandemic caused child poverty to decrease.
7. Meyer and Sullivan (2012).
8. The following data give the percentage of household annual incomes spent in recent years on food for three different income intervals: Income less than $15,000 = 28.2 percent; income between $15,000 and $30,000 = 18.2 percent; income between $30,000 and $40,000 = 16.4 percent. See also Clemens (2021).
9. This number is obtained as follows: $12,784 × (5/3) = $21,307.
10. In addition to footnote 7 above, see Meyer and Sullivan (2008, 2009, and 2011).
11. Meyer and Sullivan (2012), p. 117.
12. Meyer and Sullivan (2011).
13. See, for example, Piketty and Saez (2003) and Atkinson, Piketty and Saez (2011).
14. Piketty, Saez and Zucman (2018).
15. Matthews (2018).
16. See Geloso (2019).
17. Geloso, Magness, Moore and Schlosser (2018).
18. Piketty, Saez and Zucman (2018).
19. Auten and Splinter (2019).
20. Leonard (2022).
21. A Gini coefficient measures the degree to which the total income in a country would have to be redistributed in order for everyone to have the same income. For example, a Gini = 0 would mean that all incomes are equal and no redistribution is needed. At the other extreme, a Gini = 1 would mean that one person has all of the income, and, hence, all of this income would need to be redistributed to have equality. In sum, a higher value for the Gini implies a more unequal distribution of income.
22. Gramm and Early (2019b).
23. OECD data indicate the following Gini coefficients (and the relevant year for each measure) for each of the Nordic countries: Iceland, 2017 = .25; Norway, 2019 = .26; Denmark, 2018 = .26; Finland, 2018 = .27; and Sweden, 2019 = .28. Source: OECD (2022).
24. Barro (2000), p. 8.
25. Persson and Tabellini (1991); Alesina and Rodrik (1994).
26. Li and Zou (1998); Forbes (2000).
27. Barro (2000).
28. Banerjee and Duflo (2003).

8. International trade: magic and black magic

8.1 INTRODUCTION

Some people feel strongly about and pay much attention to news about international trade, especially when they perceive that imports might affect their lives, or the lives of loved ones. Contrastingly, many others seem oblivious to the fact that trade affects them essentially every day in a significant manner, no matter who they are.[1]

International trade is an example of specialization, and we know from Chapter 2 that specialization increases productivity and standards of living magically. On the other hand, specialization creates interdependence, and this can end up harming individuals and communities if they are highly specialized and all of a sudden there is little or no demand for what they produce (*black magic*).

Fortunately, international trade increases competition (a cause of *good magic*) which: (a) forces firms to become more efficient and/or to lower their profit margins; (b) drives inefficient firms out of business; (c) leads to better quality products; and (d) stimulates innovation. All of these benefit essentially everyone, even those who are on the losing side of specialization.

This chapter examines traditional thinking and newer ideas about how international trade affects standards of living. It focuses on balanced trade. The literature on this topic has two parts to it, namely static analysis and dynamic analysis. Static analysis is the traditional approach that dominates conventional thinking. It implicitly assumes that all firms are perfectly efficient, technology is fixed, and that there is no way to improve the quality of products. The more recent dynamic analysis allows all of the above to change in response to foreign competition.

It is likely that international trade does not reduce the standard of living for as many people as traditional thinking along static lines implies. To be sure, in the USA there are probably millions who are absolutely worse off. But there are perhaps tens of millions of Americans who feel left behind even though they are not worse off. It is just that international trade has increased their standard of living much less than it has for others.

8.2   ADAM SMITH AND DAVID RICARDO

Before proceeding to an investigation of the winners and losers from balanced international trade we need to review the origins of the idea that international trade is good for a country. Path-breaking ideas were developed by Adam Smith and David Ricardo.[2] Their ideas were directly opposed to the prevailing belief of mercantilists, who thought that international trade was a zero sum game, i.e., exports are good and imports are bad. (Does this sound familiar?) Smith first and then Ricardo second explained why all countries can gain from international trade.

Smith's ideas are called absolute advantage theory. He reasoned that if a foreign country is more productive in producing some good X, then it will produce X more cheaply than is done domestically. Hence, home consumers will be better off if they import X at the lower price. To him this was just plain old common sense.

As we know from Chapter 2, Smith explained how specialization can almost miraculously increase labor productivity. However, he pointed out that the optimum degree of specialization in producing any given product depends on the size of the market, i.e., on the total potential quantity demanded per time period for that product. For example, in the pin industry discussed in Chapter 2, it would be nonsense for a factory to specialize and produce 48,000 pins per day if the market for its pins is so small that the quantity demanded were only a few hundred pins per day.

Smith pointed out that international trade increases the size of the market for all firms. Indeed, excluding transportation costs, free trade with all nations makes the entire world a potential market. Consequently, international trade allows firms to alter their production process via incorporating a greater degree of specialization. This, in turn, increases output for each firm; hence, GDP goes up in countries engaging in international trade. An increase in GDP raises the average standard of living in each country. International trade along absolute advantage lines is not a zero sum game.[3]

David Ricardo came up with the theory of comparative advantage. His ideas very simply put are as follows. Suppose a country, say the USA, has an absolute advantage in every product, i.e., it can produce and sell everything more cheaply than any imported version of each product. Ricardo would say that the USA could gain by specializing in and exporting the products where its absolute advantage is greatest. These would be its comparative advantage products. Conversely, the USA should import those products where its absolute advantage is the least. In doing so it will be able to produce more and consume more, thereby increasing the average standard of living. Similar logic applies to foreign countries. Again, international trade is not a zero sum game.

8.3   TRADITIONAL THINKING ABOUT WINNERS AND LOSERS

8.3.1   Introduction

International trade helps consumers by providing both a larger choice of products, lower prices, and perhaps better quality. Lower prices occur for two reasons. First, the prices of imports are apt to be lower than prices at home. Second, home firms are forced to reduce their prices in order to stay competitive. Caliendo, Dvorkin, and Parro of the Federal Reserve Bank of St. Louis calculated that lower prices in the USA from its trade with China increased the US average standard of living by 6.7 percent, which is more than $2,500 per year.[4]

In addition, a scholarly study of the European Union concluded that EU firms' markups over marginal cost were significantly smaller because of the increase in competition from free trade among member countries. This meant that European prices were lower, thereby increasing the standard of living by 2 percent of GDP.[5] This was equivalent to adding hundreds of billions of euros to total incomes every year. Similarly, Feenstra and Weinstein concluded that well-being in the USA has increased because of lower profit markups induced via foreign competition.[6]

Essentially everyone knows that international trade harms domestic firms (and their workers) who compete with imports. There is much more to it than what is commonly known. For example, international trade harms people who consume products that are exported by their country. The USA exports a huge percentage of the output of many agricultural products. When the USA exports a product it means that there is less available domestically. This, in turn, tends to increase the domestic prices of the goods that are exported. The price of wheat in the USA is undoubtedly higher because of international trade. Thus, it is likely that consumers pay more for flour and for all baked goods because the country exports so much wheat. Unfortunately, we do not hear about this, primarily because we have no idea about the extent of it.

8.3.2   Static Analysis: The Short Run

In the static analysis of the effects of international trade, the short run refers to the time interval during which imports cause some domestic firms to downsize or shut down, and workers to be laid-off. Thus, in the short run, imports harm workers who lose their jobs and the owners of firms that lose money and/or shut down. This might also harm workers who accept a lower wage rate or salary in order to keep their jobs. On the other hand, in the short run, exports are good for the workers and owners of firms who produce the exported products. Profits, wages, and salaries are apt to be higher, and jobs are more secure in export industries. Clearly, this is not rocket science!

8.3.3 Static Analysis: The Long Run

The long run refers to a time interval that is long enough for any resources that were displaced by imports to be fully employed again. In the real world this is probably many years. The assumption is that laid-off workers have found a job somewhere and once-idle factories and stores have been revamped and are being used again.

A classic scholarly paper by Stolper and Samuelson is a huge part of the conventional wisdom on the static winners and losers from international trade in the long run.[7] Their major conclusion is known as the Stolper-Samuelson theorem. What it says, in brief, is that the resources (labor or capital) used intensively in the production of exports will gain at the expense of the resources used intensively to produce the imported goods. Rigorously speaking, this conclusion means that the real incomes of the winners will increase relative to the real incomes of the losers. But in a practical sense, this usually has been taken to mean that the losers will be absolutely worse off.

The USA imports products from Asia and Latin America that are produced with low wage unskilled labor and/or with low tech capital. These were only 9 percent of US manufacturing imports in 1991 but increased to 28 percent by 2007 after China was admitted to the World Trade Organization.[8] Contrastingly, America exports many manufacturing products such as commercial jets and earth moving equipment; these use much skilled labor (especially engineers) and high-tech capital.

Unskilled labor is usually defined to include workers with a high school degree or less who are not officially certified as a skilled craftsperson such as a plumber, carpenter, electrician, etc. Low-tech capital can be loosely defined as any tools or assembly line machinery that can easily be duplicated in a third world country. Examples include the machinery used in many foreign textile mills and glass factories.

The Stolper-Samuelson theorem hypothetically assumes that any workers who initially lose their jobs, and any factories that shut down because of imports will eventually be fully employed. Applying this theorem to the USA means that any unskilled workers who become unemployed in the import competing industries will eventually find jobs either in the export industries or elsewhere.

In the USA the contracting import competing industries release much more unskilled labor and low-tech capital than are needed in the expanding export industries. Contrastingly, the expanding export industries will need much more skilled labor and high-tech capital goods than are available. Thus, wage rates for unskilled labor (and rates of return for owners of low-tech capital) will go down relative to the wage rates for skilled labor and rates of return for owners of high-tech capital.[9] This is the Stolper-Samuelson theorem as applied to the USA.

This theorem applies to unskilled workers no matter where they work, even in the export industry. Presumably, a worker who pushes a broom in one of Boeing's factories will have a relatively lower wage rate because of international trade, even though Boeing is a big-time exporter. Furthermore, the Stolper-Samuelson theorem implies that all skilled workers in the USA (e.g., engineers) will be relatively better off from international trade even if they work in an import competing industry – provided they still have a job.

8.3.4   More on the Long Run Losers from International Trade

Free trade causes dislocation for a few in order to benefit all. The personal hardships that result are often severe and must be alleviated.[10]

A story
At one time, the western PA town of about 11,000 people where I grew up had seven busy glass factories. The town was prosperous, but everything depended on the buying power of those who worked in the glass factories. Eventually, all seven glass factories closed because of intense competition from imports. Many blue-collar workers lost not only their jobs, but also their pensions.[11] Furthermore, the harm spread throughout the town like a disease, i.e., stores shut down, and many doctors, dentists, accountants, lawyers, and other professionals could no longer survive there.

When a town or a region specializes in one industry and that industry dies because of imports, then: (a) incomes fall and spending decreases (Say's Law), and (b) stores as well as professional service providers disappear (Keynes' Law and Leontief's Law). Such events have happened in Wooster, Ohio (from imports of plastic kitchen containers), Youngstown, Ohio (from imports of steel) and in Detroit (from imports of motor vehicles). Economic black magic!

Until John Kennedy initiated (and Congress passed) the Trade Expansion Act of 1962, the USA had no federal program to help workers who were displaced by imports.[12] Since that time there have been many additions and revisions to this law that extend unemployment benefits, subsidize wage rates of workers 50 or older, help retrain displaced workers and move them to areas where jobs exist, etc. Such changes occurred in 1974, 1981, 2002, 2010, and 2011.[13]

In 2020 the federal government transferred more than $500 million to states who administer these programs. This, however, amounts to roughly 0.025

percent of the USA's GDP. Denmark spends 20 times the US percentage helping unemployed people get jobs, while France and Germany each spend about five times the US percentage.[14] Perhaps even more importantly, there is little or no help for entire communities that have been devastated by international trade.

8.4   DYNAMIC GAINS FROM TRADE

In the existing international trade literature, there is a good deal of consensus about the significance of the static welfare gains from trade. In contrast, there is much less consensus about the importance of the dynamic gains from international trade.[15]

The dynamic gains from international trade arise as a result of increased foreign competition. Economists have been aware of dynamic gains for a long time, but only recently have they attempted to quantify the magnitude of such gains. I suspect that someday we might realize that the static gains from trade (i.e., primarily lower prices) are relatively small compared to the dynamic gains.[16]

As pointed out above, traditional trade theories typically assume that firms are perfectly efficient, but there is much evidence that this simply is not true. International trade means that home firms face increased competition from firms all over the world. One response to more foreign competition is that home firms strive to reduce production costs via a greater degree of efficiency. When this occurs, then labor productivity goes up. If productivity increases, then output and standards of living increase.

One example of this deals with Chile when it opened its economy to foreign trade in the 1970s. One scholarly study concluded that the increase in foreign competition induced Chilean firms who competed with imports to increase their efficiency from 3 percent to 10 percent *more* than efficiency increased elsewhere in the economy.[17]

Another example deals with the American iron ore industry in the 1980s when it faced strong competition from iron ore firms in Brazil. The workers in the US firms agreed to changing the labor contract rules to allow for more flexibility. For example, equipment operators were allowed to do routine maintenance, instead of restricting such work to the official repair workers. Within a few years, labor productivity doubled in the US iron ore producers.[18]

Also, international trade increases average labor productivity domestically via its effect on the *structure* of domestic production. To explain, imports cause the least productive home firms to contract or go out of business. More productive home firms survive and expand, i.e., Economic Darwinism at work. This shift in resources from lower to higher productivity firms increases the average productivity in a country.[19]

Competition from China prompted reallocation of output from low innovators to high innovators in Europe, that accounted for 14 percent of European technology upgrading from 2000–2007. Also, it has been estimated that at least 25 percent of the growth in productivity in some years in the USA occurred via this mechanism.[20]

Perhaps the most important reason why international trade generates dynamic gains deals with the effect of greater foreign competition on advances in technology and innovations. There are many studies that document that this happens. Some examples are: Bartell et al. on American valve makers; Freeman and Kleiner on footwear; and Bugamelli et al. on Italian manufacturing.[21] A study for the entire EU by Bloom et al. concludes that Chinese import competition led to a sharp increase in innovation and productivity in textile companies who felt threatened by China.[22]

It should be noted, however, that not all scholarly studies agree. For example, Autor et al. found that industries in America that were most affected by Chinese imports, tended to have fewer US patents for several years after China joined the WTO.[23] If new patents are positively correlated with innovations, then this study is inconsistent with the others cited here.

Comment

Increased foreign competition can induce domestic firms to shape up, e.g., become more efficient, produce better quality products, and innovate more. These dynamic gains help everyone. Consequently, some of the so-called losers from trade via the static analysis of the Stolper-Samuelson theorem might conceivably be better off, i.e., they are losers in a relative sense (compared to those who have gained much) but not in an absolute sense. If this were true it would indeed represent an example of economic magic. Unfortunately, we do not know the extent of the dynamic gains from trade at the macroeconomic level.

NOTES

1. Hochberg (2020), p. xv.
2. Smith (1776) and Ricardo (1817).
3. Smith was not aware of the concept of economies of scale, wherein the average cost per unit and the selling price decrease as the size of the firm and its output go up. The larger market for a firm's product created by international trade can create economies of scale.
4. Caliendo, Dvorkin and Parro (2015).
5. Veld (2019).
6. Feenstra and Weinstein (2017).
7. Stolper and Samuelson (1941). Their ideas were extended by Jones and Scheinkman (1977).
8. Autor, Dorn and Hanson (2013).

9. The Stolper-Samuelson theorem does not refer to rates of return to capital, because this is not conceptually similar to wage rates for labor. The appropriate measure for the incomes of owners of capital goods is 'rental rates', as for example the rental rates for cars and trucks or for copy machines. There is always an implicit rental rate for any capital good, even if the firm owns it.

10. Fred Bergsten, as quoted in Allen (2016), p. 3.

11. Firms could legally borrow the funds that workers paid into their pensions. When a firm went bankrupt it did not have to repay the loans.

12. The 1933 Reciprocal Trade Ageements Act allows the President to levy high tariffs on imports that have substantially harmed American workers and/or firms, but it has no provision to directly help those who are harmed.

13. Semuels (2018).

14. US Department of Labor (2020), p. 46.

15. Melitz and Redding (2021).

16. This statement is consistent with the point of view in Melitz and Redding (2014).

17. Pavcnik (2002).

18. Chatterjee (2005).

19. Melitz (2003) and Melitz and Redding (2013).

20. For the USA see Foster, Haltiwanger and Krizan (2001).

21. Bartel, Ichniowski and Shaw (2007); Freeman and Kleiner (2005); Bugamelli, Schivardi and Zizza (2008).

22. Bloom, Draca and van Reenen (2016).

23. Autor, Dorn, Hanson, Pisano and Shu (2016).

9. Trade deficits and jobs: economic magic

9.1 INTRODUCTION

This chapter examines how exports, imports, foreign investments in the USA, and trade balance deficits have affected employment in the USA. First it considers the myth that imports always decrease GDP. Then it examines scholarly studies on job losses associated with imports from China. Next, it considers total jobs in the USA associated with international trade. After this, it looks at American jobs in foreign firms operating in the USA, and jobs created by foreign portfolio investment in the USA.

Perhaps most importantly, this chapter provides a rough estimate of the employment created indirectly by the net capital inflows that equal the trade balance and current account deficits. Jobs are created because the annual net capital inflow helps to finance domestic investment and economic growth. The tentative conclusion is that these net capital inflows significantly offset the direct loss of jobs from excessive imports. Moreover, it is conceivable that the overall net effect of current account deficits and the equal in magnitude net capital inflows might be more jobs! If so, then this is, indeed, economic magic!

Finally, the chapter reviews two perspectives dealing with the underlying cause of chronic trade deficits. One perspective is microeconomic in nature and the other represents a macroeconomic approach. The chapter makes a first attempt to reconcile these.

9.2 MISLEADING STATEMENTS IN THE MEDIA

Many people believe that imports always reduce GDP and cause a loss of jobs. Here are two media statements along these lines:[1]

> Trade was the biggest drag on the economy during the spring, subtracting 3.5 percentage points from growth.[2]

> When imports outpace exports, more jobs go to overseas workers than to U.S. workers ... The widening of the trade deficit cut one-half percentage point from overall growth last year.[3]

These media accounts reflect a lack of understanding as to how the government calculates GDP. It does not measure output directly. Rather it first measures what Americans buy, both domestically produced goods and services as well as imports.[4] These include consumer goods (C), capital goods used for domestic investment in structures and equipment (I), and government purchases of goods and services (G). To this it adds the value of US exports (Ex). The values for C, I, G, and Ex include imports. In order to calculate GDP, the government subtracts imports (Im) from C + I + G + Ex, as in Equation (9.1).

$$GDP = C + I + G + Ex - Im \qquad (9.1)$$

The fact that imports, Im, appear with a negative sign makes it look like imports always reduce GDP. However, this is not true. For example, suppose that imports go up, say, by $500 billion from one year to another, but American purchases of goods and services produced in the USA stay the same. Then the sum of C + I + G + Ex would be $500 billion larger. However, the government would subtract the larger import number from this sum, and we would end up with the same value for GDP.

The value for imports, in itself, does not directly affect the value for GDP. However, an increase in imports will reduce GDP if home purchases of domestic goods and services go down by the increase in imports. That is, if people substitute imports for home produced goods. Chapter 4 showed that, typically, just the opposite happens. Imports rise simultaneously with increased purchases of home goods and services.

9.3   THE BALANCE OF TRADE VERSUS THE CURRENT ACCOUNT BALANCE

Equation (9.2) indicates that the Current Account (CA) is the balance of trade (BT) plus [net international earnings] and [net international gifts]. Net international earnings are what American workers and firms earn abroad minus what foreign workers and firms earn in the USA. This has been positive in recent decades. Net International gifts

$$CA = BT + [net international earnings] + [net international gifts] \qquad (9.2)$$

are gifts received by Americans from foreigners minus gifts by Americans to foreigners. The latter includes US government foreign aid. Net international gifts are almost always negative, i.e., we give more than we get. Hence, [net int'l earnings] and [net int'l gifts] tend to offset each other, but end up net positive. This, however, is small in absolute value compared to the huge negative values for the balance of trade.

The solid line in Figure 9.1 shows the US balance of trade (BT), i.e., exports minus imports, from 1990 through 2017. It has been negative in all years but one over this interval. The dashed line in Figure 9.1 shows the US Current Account (CA) over the same interval. Clearly, the CA and the BT lines have moved very closely together.

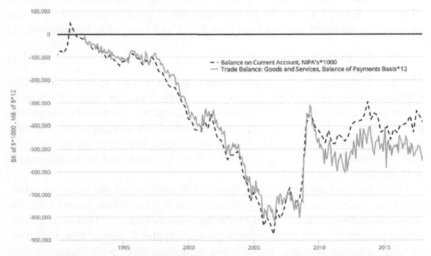

Source: US Bureau of Economic Analysis, Balance on Current Account, NIPA's [NETFI], retrieved from FRED, Federal Reserve Bank of St. Louis; https://fred.stlouisfed.org/series/NETFI.

Figure 9.1   US trade balance and current account balance 1990–2017

9.4   SCHOLARLY STUDIES ON JOB LOSSES FROM TRADE WITH CHINA

There have been many excellent studies dealing with the loss of jobs, primarily in manufacturing, associated with US imports from China. Figure 9.2 shows that manufacturing employment as a percentage of total US employment has decreased steadily from 38 percent in December 1945 to 8.5 percent in December 2019. Two facts are noteworthy. First, the decline occurred for more than 30 years before 1980, during which time the trade balance and current account were roughly zero. Thus, during this interval the decrease in the percentage of manufacturing employment cannot be blamed on excessive imports.

Second, the slope of this curve does not change appreciably between 1990 and 2009 during which the CA and trade balance decreased steadily. Although these facts prove nothing rigorously, they make one suspicious about the hypothesis that trade deficits have caused significant decreases in manufacturing relative employment.

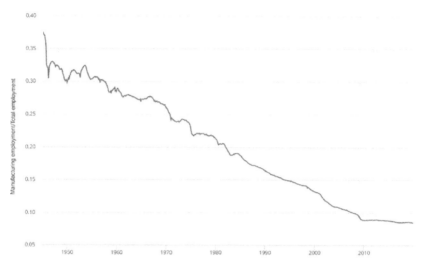

Source: US Bureau of Labor Statistics, All Employees, Manufacturing [MANEMP], retrieved from FRED, Federal Reserve Bank of St. Louis; https://fred.stlouisfed.org/series/MANEMP.

Figure 9.2   Manufacturing employment percentage 1945–2019

Figure 9.3 indicates that the *level* of manufacturing employment increased from 12.5 million after World War Two to 19.4 million in September 1979. This is true even though the percentage of total employment in manufacturing was falling steadily. It is only since 1979 that jobs in manufacturing have decreased in an absolute sense. This decrease was gradual until about the year 2000, and became more rapid from then until 2010. This more rapid decline occurred after China was admitted to the World Trade Organization (WTO) on 11 December 2001. After 2010, however, manufacturing employment increased by about 1.5 million jobs until the end of 2019. This happened even though the USA continued to import heavily from China.

A study by Autor, Dorn, and Hanson[5] (which has been cited roughly 1,000 times) closely examines the effect of Chinese imports on US employment. They say: 'Hence, we estimate that rising exposure to Chinese import competition explains … 44% of the decline [in manufacturing employment] for the full 1990 through 2007 period.'[6] The decrease in manufacturing employment of 44 percent from 1990 through 2007 amounted to about 1.6 million jobs.

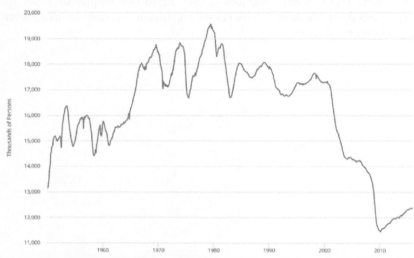

Source: US Bureau of Labor Statistics, All Employees, Manufacturing [MANEMP], retrieved
from FRED, Federal Reserve Bank of St. Louis; https://fred.stlouisfed.org/series/MANEMP.

Figure 9.3   US manufacturing employees 1950–2015

Another scholarly paper is that of Caliendo, Dvorkin and Parro (CDP) of the
Federal Reserve Bank of St. Louis.[7] They use a sophisticated general equilibrium model for 38 countries and the 50 US states to simulate the effects of
imports from China (between 2000 and 2007) on manufacturing employment
in each of the 50 states. Their model contains an input–output table; hence,
they attempt to capture the upstream loss in jobs associated with Leontief's
Law. That is, when a US firm downsized or shut down this affected employment in the industries that previously supplied that firm. They find that imports
from China over this (relatively brief) time interval resulted in a net loss of just
under one million jobs.

Chapter 8 pointed out that CDP also calculate the gain to well-being in the
USA from the lower prices associated with trading with China. The details
are worth repeating. Lower prices occurred because of: (a) cheaper Chinese
products, and (b) lower prices for American products as a result of the increase
in international competition from China. They conclude that the lower prices
generated a 6.7 percent increase in the average US standard of living.

Personal income per person in the USA in 2007 was just under $40,000, and
6.7 percent of this is more than $2,500. Consequently, the lower prices associ-
ated with more trade with China allegedly cost more than 1 million jobs from

2000–2007, but, allegedly again, it increased the average standard of living by about $2,500 per year.

A more recent estimate of jobs lost via trade with China is that of Scott and Mokhiber who say: 'The growth of the US trade deficit with China between 2001 and 2018 was responsible for the loss of 3.7 million US jobs.'[8] The 3.7 million jobs lost is much larger than the other estimates given above. The bottom line is that US trade with China has *directly* reduced manufacturing jobs in America by somewhere between a little over one million and almost four million. My guess is that it is closer to four million.

9.5   TOTAL JOBS RELATED TO US IMPORTS AND EXPORTS

Laura M. Baughman and Joseph F. Francois have calculated the total number of jobs supported directly and indirectly by US exports and imports. They use a complex computable general equilibrium model of the US economy that includes an input–output table (along the lines of Leontief's Law) and so-called multiplier effects that reflect increases in spending from the extra income earned by those having new jobs (along the lines of Say's Law and Keynes' Law).[9] Thus, they attempt to model the complex nature of our economy as explained in Chapter 3 above, and conclude that: 'most analysts … miss the largest source of job-creating activity that comes from trade: the extra spending power [that] … generates still more job-supporting economic activity'.[10] The jobs related to imports include: (a) unloading imports at docks and airports; (b) transporting imports from a port to a warehouse and then to retail stores; (c) jobs at the warehouses; (d) jobs at the retail level handling the sale and service of the imports. Perhaps most importantly, their calculations take account of jobs gained as well as jobs lost via international trade, i.e., they get an estimate of *net* jobs.[11]

Baughman and Francois conclude that the net number of jobs in the USA related to international trade as of 2017 was approximately 39 million, which was slightly more than 25 percent of total nonfarm employment in that year. Most of these, 36 million, were in services. These include jobs in construction, wholesale and retail trade, personal and recreation services, and other services such as health and education. They arise because Say's Law and Keynes' Law imply that any new jobs generate extra income and this leads to extra spending on items like eating out, day care, or pre-care for young children, travel and home renovation projects.[12]

9.6   JOBS FROM FOREIGN FIRMS IN THE USA

Richards and Schaefer[13] in the International Trade Administration of the US Department of Commerce have done a rigorous analysis of American jobs in 2013 as a consequence of foreign direct investment (FDI), i.e., foreign purchases of productive facilities in the USA. Their study used the US Applied General Equilibrium model. Thus, it attempts to capture the extreme complexity of the US economy.

The increase in US employment from FDI was broken down into three components. The first was 6.1 million jobs for those who work directly in the US affiliates of foreign firms. Second, 2.4 million jobs were generated indirectly: (a) upstream via jobs in the firms that supply inputs to the US affiliates of foreign firms, as determined by an input/output table, and (b) two types of downstream jobs, i.e., (i) workers in the foreign firms' distribution chains, and (ii) those jobs stimulated by the higher spending induced by the increased incomes of all workers involved. Third, 3.5 million jobs were created by productivity growth in American firms from spillovers of advances in technology in the foreign firms. This gave a total of 12 million jobs generated by FDI.

9.7   JOBS ASSOCIATED WITH FOREIGN PORTFOLIO INVESTMENT IN THE USA

Foreign funds flowing into the USA can be broken down into two categories, namely FDI (as described above) and foreign portfolio investment (FPI). The latter involves foreign purchases of financial assets like stocks, bonds, etc. from Americans, and the placement of foreign funds in US banks. This section first examines the cumulative magnitudes (not the annual flows) of different types of FPI, and then it explains how these have helped to create jobs.

The cumulative magnitude of foreign portfolio investment is enormous! Table 9.1 shows the financial assets (and their composition) of the 24 countries who had $168 billion or more of US financial assets at the end of June 2019. Japan held the most, $2.28 trillion. The total for these 24 and all other countries was $20.5 trillion.

Foreign holdings of long-term treasury bonds were $5.9 trillion – roughly 30 percent of the Federal government's long-term debt in 2019. Warnock and Warnock conclude that China's purchases (alone) of US government bonds have, at times, reduced the 10-year Treasury bond yield by 80 or 90 basis points, i.e., by almost one percentage point.[14] In 2019 China's holdings of $1.11 trillion of long-term Treasury bonds was slightly less than 20 percent of total foreign holdings. Consequently, the overall reduction in US interest

Table 9.1   *Foreign holdings of US securities, June 2019 (billions of dollars)*

Country	Total	Equities	LT Treas. bonds	Agency	Corp bonds	ST debt
Japan	2,280	596	1,065	297	260	62
Cayman Islands	1,877	1,084	134	35	524	99
UK	1,776	1,002	286	8	422	58
China	1,543	189	1,109	227	14	4
Canada	1,262	956	99	6	184	16
Ireland	1,081	456	224	46	251	105
Switzerland	813	450	195	11	117	41
Belgium	780	58	175	6	515	27
Taiwan	626	68	172	266	117	4
Norway	452	309	98	–	45	1
Netherlands	421	284	46	14	73	3
Hong Kong	397	110	190	13	55	13
Germany	396	191	69	5	120	11
France	373	177	114	3	60	19
South Korea	366	153	111	43	52	7
Singapore	363	180	133	5	33	12
Bermuda	349	111	49	29	134	26
Australia	344	262	33	4	36	8
Brazil	322	5	309	3	1	3
Saudi Arabia	289	93	130	6	14	46
Kuwait	287	197	38	7	21	25
Sweden	236	180	49	–	6	1
Virgin Islands	178	112	27	2	23	14
India	168	4	161	–	–	2
Other	1,930	739	705	63	226	197
TOTAL	20,534	8,630	5,903	1,145	3,943	913

Source: Report on Foreign Portfolio Holdings of US Securities: June 2019, US Dept of Treasury, 30 April 2020.

rates from all FPI was undoubtedly greater (perhaps much greater) than a one percentage point reduction. We simply do not know.

Mortgage interest rates and corporate bond rates have typically moved up and down with the 10-year treasury bond interest rate. Lower mortgage rates stimulate the construction and purchase of new houses and apartments, and expansions by small businesses. Lower corporate bond rates induce firms to increase domestic nonresidential investment. All of these activities create jobs in construction and, more importantly, permanent jobs in stores, factories and office buildings.

Next, Table 9.2 shows the values (as of 30 March 2020) of foreign owned deposits in the 14 US banks where such deposits exceeded $100 million. JP Morgan Chase Bank had an astounding $51.3 billion of such deposits. Citibank, and Bank of America had foreign deposits of $29.5 billion and $22.7 billion, respectively. Total foreign deposits in the top 14 banks were about $136 billion. Banks typically lend most of the funds deposited with them, and many of these loans finance household purchases of real estate and consumer durables, as well as small business expansions or startups. All of these activities create jobs.

Table 9.2   *Foreign deposits in US banks, 30 March 2020 (billions of dollars)*

Bank	Foreign deposits
JP Morgan Chase	51.26
Citibank	29.50
Bank of America	22.71
Bank of New York Mellon	13.50
Deutsche Bank Trust Co America	7.12
HSBC Bank USA	6.46
Wells Fargo Bank	3.20
BMO Harris Bank	0.72
Mizuho Bank (USA)	0.59
Bank of China	0.40
MUFG Union Bank	0.26
BAC Florida Bank	0.23
Barclay's Bank Delaware	0.13
Habib American Bank	0.11
TOTAL	136.19

We have no idea about the magnitude of jobs created by FPI, but it could be substantial. However, American firms investing abroad and US investors buying foreign stocks, bonds, etc. have indirectly reduced employment in the USA. Thus, the perhaps millions of American jobs associated with FPI and FDI in the USA tell us nothing about the net gain or loss in jobs from all international investment activities.

9.8   HAVE TRADE BALANCE DEFICITS INDIRECTLY INCREASED JOBS?

The net outflow of dollars to purchase imports ... are offset each year by a net ... purchase [of] US assets. This capital surplus stimulates the US economy while boosting our productive capacity.[15]

None of the studies reviewed above tell us anything about the net gain or loss of American jobs via: (a) current account deficits reducing employment, and (b) matching net capital inflows increasing employment by stimulating economic growth. The above quotation makes it clear that the ideas in this section are not new. However, to my knowledge, no one has attempted to obtain an estimate of the number of jobs gained indirectly via the capital inflows that match our current account deficits. The truth is that our economy might be too complex to figure this out rigorously. Nevertheless, this section makes a modest rough attempt at this.

9.8.1   Domestic Saving, Domestic Investment, and the Current Account Balance

Figure 9.4 shows domestic investment (the thick line) and domestic saving (the thin line) from 1970 until 1998. Domestic saving equals the sum of: (a) household saving; (b) business saving; and (c) government saving. If the government experiences a budget surplus, then this adds to domestic saving; it subtracts if the government has a budget deficit.

Before the mid-1980s the two lines moved very closely together; domestic saving was, in general, sufficient to finance total domestic investment. Figure 9.4 indicates that since about 1984 total domestic investment has generally been greater than total saving. The absolute value for the difference has been exactly equal to the absolute value for the US current account (CA).

Since the early 1970s, the US and other major countries have had a system of flexible exchange rates.[16] This means that exchange rates adjust 24/7 to ensure that each country's total international sales always equal its total international purchases. For the USA this means that its current account deficits are matched by its net sales of assets, i.e., a net capital inflow. Consequently, the excess of domestic investment over total domestic saving has been financed in recent decades by the net inflow of foreign savings!

9.8.2   Some Back of the Envelope Calculations

This section makes the perhaps heroic assumption that [jobs created per $1 billion of domestic net investment] are the same as [jobs created per $1 billion

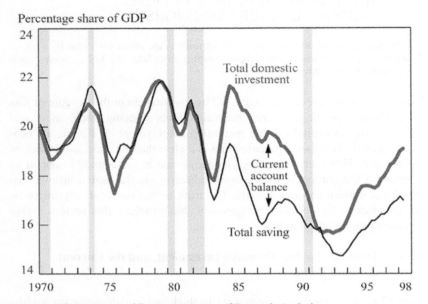

Percentage share of GDP

Source: US Department of Commerce, Bureau of Economic Analysis.

Figure 9.4   US saving, investment and current account 1970–1998

of net capital inflow]. The objective is to get some kind of a very rough estimate of the jobs created indirectly via the net capital inflows that match the
CA deficits.

Cumulative net domestic investment in the USA from 1990 through 2005
was approximately $10.5 trillion.[17] This represents the cumulative addition to
the US capital stock over this time interval. The cumulative value for the US
current account over this same time interval was about −$4.4 trillion. This
means that the matching cumulative net capital inflow into the US over this
interval was +$4.4 trillion.

Total nonfarm employment in the US from 1990 through 2005 increased
by 25.9 million.[18] Because the capital stock increased by $10.5 trillion, this
implies that every $1 billion of new capital goods was associated with an
increase of 0.002467 million new jobs. This is 2,467 jobs per $1 billion of new
capital stock.

If [jobs per $1 billion of net capital inflow] were the same as [jobs per $1
billion of domestic net investment], then the cumulative net capital inflow of
$4.4 trillion would have generated 10.85 million new jobs from 1990–2005.[19]
This is slightly more than 40 percent of the total increase in jobs over this

interval! Consequently, it is conceivable that the capital inflows have indirectly helped the US economy grow faster and, hence, have created almost 11 million jobs.[20]

In order to obtain an estimate of the overall net change in jobs from CA deficits and accompanying net capital inflows, these 10.8 million new jobs must be compared with the millions of jobs lost directly via excessive imports. From 1990 until approximately 2008, the US annual trade deficits (goods and services) with China grew steadily more negative from roughly zero to $250 billion.

Contrastingly, the US trade deficits with all other countries went from about $100 billion to slightly worse than $500 billion over this same time interval.[21] Thus, three million to four million jobs lost via excessive imports from China were likely less than half of all jobs lost. It seems reasonable to assume that the total jobs lost *directly* from excessive imports were somewhere in the six million to eight million range.

The estimate of 10.85 million jobs gained via net capital inflow overstates the true number if a significant percentage of the net inflow was not eventually used to finance domestic investment. Another source of imprecision comes from the assumption here that [jobs created by $1 billion of net capital inflow] equal [jobs created by $1 billion of domestic net investment]. Clearly, the 10.85 million new jobs should be taken with a grain of salt.

The point here is that: (a) a large number of jobs has probably been created indirectly via the net capital inflow; (b) it is not unreasonable to believe that this significantly offset the jobs lost directly via current account deficits; and (c) it is conceivable that the overall net effect has been an increase in jobs! We simply do not know! All of this illustrates the idea of economic magic.

9.9   CAUSES OF CHRONIC TRADE AND CURRENT ACCOUNT DEFICITS

Many reasons have been given for the chronic US balance of trade and current account deficits. Two of these are correct. One of them involves a microeconomic perspective, and the other a macroeconomic perspective. To my knowledge, no one has attempted to reconcile these.

9.9.1   Two Perspectives on the Cause of US Current Account Deficits

The *microeconomic* perspective on this issue focuses on one market, the FX market. As pointed out above, the USA and other major affluent countries operate on a system of flexible exchange rates. Consequently, the USA's excessive purchases of goods and services (the negative CA) is always matched by asset sales internationally that exceed asset purchases (the positive net capital inflow).

Foreign investors apparently love US corporate stocks and bonds, and US government bonds. Also, foreign firms and wealthy people want to keep large sums of money in American banks. Finally, foreign firms want to build and buy productive facilities in the USA, and wealthy foreign households want to own houses and other real estate in America.

When foreigners buy dollars in order to purchase US assets, this appreciates the value of the dollar in FX markets; it takes more yen, British pounds, or euros to buy one dollar. Conversely, it takes fewer dollars to buy FX; hence, the dollar prices of products from Japan, the UK, the EU go down. Consequently, the quantity of US imports increases.

Also, when the dollar appreciates, the foreign currency prices of American products increase, and this reduces the quantity of US exports. In sum, the net capital inflow each year keeps the FX value for the dollar relatively high; this, in turn, stimulates imports, and reduces exports, thereby helping to cause the trade balance and current account to be negative. This represents the *microeconomic* perspective.

The second correct reason for the US trade and current account deficits takes a *macroeconomic* perspective. The current account (CA) equals domestic saving (Sv) minus domestic investment (I), as in Figure 9.4 and equation (9.3a). It can be proven that a country's (Sv − I) always equals that country's total income minus total purchases. Thus, equation (9.3a) can be written as in equation (9.3b), where total purchases are the sum of consumption (C), investment in new capital goods (I), and government purchases (G).[22]

$$CA = Sv - I \hspace{8cm} (9.3a)$$

$$CA = \text{Total Income} - (C + I + G) \hspace{4cm} (9.3b)$$

Equation (9.3b) gives the macroeconomic reason for current account deficits. A country will have a current account deficit if it is spending more, (C + I + G), than its total income, i.e., if the country is living beyond its means. This is equivalent to the fact that a budget deficit for a household means that the family has been living beyond its means. America has been living beyond its means for more than 40 years now. Household saving rates are relatively low compared to other leading nations, and the government has had chronic budget deficits.

9.9.2   Reconciling the Micro and Macro Approaches to the Deficits

The large net capital inflows each year are similar to a family receiving unsolicited blank checks from a bank that urge their use to borrow and spend, usually with a zero interest rate for 15 months. The blank checks amount to an enticement to: (a) buy now and pay later; and (b) pay much less because of a zero interest rate.

Similarly, the unsolicited net capital inflow of hundreds of billions of dollars in foreign saving each year gives the USA the ability to buy now (excessive imports) and pay later (when foreigners earn interest and profits on their investments in the USA). This provides an impetus for the USA to live beyond its means.

Furthermore, as just pointed out, the net capital inflows appreciate the dollar, thereby making imports cheaper. Also, the net capital inflows reduce US interest rates. Both events induce Americans to spend more. This is the macroeconomic equivalent to blank checks with zero interest rates enticing households to live it up.

In sum, the exogenous event of annual foreign purchases of US assets serves to reconcile the microeconomic perspective for CA deficits (the dollar appreciates) and the macroeconomic perspective (the US is living beyond its means).[23]

9.10   POSTSCRIPT

The important conclusion that trade and CA deficits might possibly have a net positive effect on domestic employment needs to be understood logically.[24]

*   Excessive imports directly cause a loss of jobs when domestic firms either shut down or downsize.
*   With a system of flexible exchange rates (as exists for the USA) the CA and trade deficits are always accompanied by a net capital inflow of equal magnitude. This helps to finance domestic investment, which means that the home country grows more rapidly, thereby creating jobs.
*   Furthermore, in a closed economy (no international trade) domestic investment cannot increase unless resources are freed up via a reduction in the production of consumer goods and/or goods for the government. More capital goods (structures and equipment) cannot be produced unless fewer other goods are produced.
*   But in an open economy, a trade balance deficit can enable domestic investment to increase (more capital goods) with no decrease in consumption or government goods.

- The country can import capital goods. Alternatively, it can import consumer and government goods, thereby freeing up domestic resources to produce more capital goods. Of course, it can do a little of both.
- We do not know what the overall net effect on jobs from the chronic US trade and CA deficits has been. However, the superior performance of the US economy compared to other leading nations, and the almost half a century record low unemployment rate at the end of 2019 strongly imply that it is simply a myth that 'excessive imports have caused a net loss of jobs'!

NOTES

1. These quotations appear in Griswold (2011), p. 2.
2. CBS News, 14 October 2010.
3. Associated Press, 11 February 2011.
4. An adjustment is made for changes in inventories.
5. Autor, Dorn and Hanson (2013).
6. Ibid., p. 2139.
7. Caliendo, Dvorkin and Parro (2015). A good nontechnical summary of this is Riquier (2017).
8. Scott and Mokhiber (2020).
9. Their analysis assumes that any increase in demand for goods and services will be satisfied by firms, i.e., Keynes' Law.
10. Baughman and Francois (2019), pp. 7–8.
11. Ibid, p. 6.
12. Ibid, p. 8.
13. Richards and Schaefer (2016).
14. Warnock and Warnock (2006).
15. Griswold (2011), p. 1.
16. Currently, this includes Canada, the EU, Japan, the UK, and Switzerland. From the early 1970s until the introduction of the euro, flexible exchange rates existed between the US dollar, Canadian dollar, Japanese yen, British pound, German mark, French franc, Italian lira, and Swiss franc.
17. FRED: Net Domestic Investment: US Bureau of Economic Analysis.
18. FRED: All Employees, Total Nonfarm: US Bureau of Labor Statistics.
19. [2,467 jobs/$billion] × [4,400 $billion] = $10.855 million jobs.
20. Note that the estimate of 10.85 million jobs created indirectly via the cumulative net capital inflow can also be obtained as follows. The $4.4 trillion of cumulative net capital inflow was enough to finance about 41.9 percent of the $10.5 trillion of net investment. Thus, 41.9 percent of 25.9 million new jobs from 1990 through 2005 equals 10.85 million jobs as a result of the net capital inflow.
21. Source: The World Bank; Federal Reserve Bank of St. Louis online at: https: www.stlouis.org/on-the-economy/2020/February/us-trade-imbalances-china -others.
22. Total saving (Sv) in (9.3a) is 'private Sv' plus government saving (govt Sv). Thus, (9.3a) can be written as:

$$CA = Sv - I = \{(private\ Sv + govt\ Sv) - I\} = \{private\ Sv - I\} + govt\ Sv.$$

Government saving is net tax revenue (net Tx) minus government purchases of goods and services (G), i.e., govt Sv = net Tx − G. Also, private Sv is total income minus net taxes and consumption, (total income − net Tx − C). Inserting these definitions into the above equation yields

CA = {(total income − net Tx − C) − I} + (net Tx − G)

This is equation (9.3b). (Note: total income is (income from productive activity in the USA by American firms and workers) + (net international income) + (net international gifts)).)

23. The critical issue is whether or not foreign purchases of US assets are exogenous or are dependent on US current account deficits. Economists distinguish between *exogenous* and *induced* net capital inflows. When foreigners accept dollars in payment for US imports, this represents an induced capital inflow for the USA. If none of these dollars were used to buy US assets (i.e., if the dollars stayed abroad) then the net capital inflow for the USA would still equal the CA deficit, but this induced capital inflow would not finance any US domestic investment. On the other hand, *exogenous* capital inflows refer to foreign purchases of US stocks, bonds, productive facilities, real estate, as well as deposits in US banks that are independent of US current account deficits, i.e., they occur simply because foreigners want to own American assets. Flexible exchange rates ensure that the value for exogenous net capital inflows equals the CA deficits. Hence, exogenous net capital inflows help to finance domestic investment and stimulate economic growth.

24. This possibility is related to the conclusion that trade deficits can increase a country's well-being by providing more present goods and more future goods. See Miller (1968) and Craighead and Miller (2010).

10. The Great Depression: economic black magic I

10.1 INTRODUCTION

The Great Depression of the 1930s is a perfect example of economic black magic. At that time no one understood why everything went south. People blamed it on labor unions, or the greedy capitalists or the damn communists. Those who had read Karl Marx said that the Great Depression was exactly what he had predicted.

The conventional thinking at that time had very little understanding about macroeconomics, perhaps because economics at that time was essentially microeconomics. As pointed out in Chapter 1, unfortunately, microeconomic theories still permeate some aspects of current macroeconomic thinking. We learned this in earlier chapters with regard to: (a) the belief that higher minimum wage rates always generate a net decrease in employment; and (b) the net effect of trade balance deficits is always a decrease in jobs.

Since the Great Depression we have learned much about macroeconomics. In this chapter we review some important facts about the Great Depression and many of the known reasons for it. Hopefully, this disaster was a unique combination of bad luck, fear, and stupid economic policies that resulted from ignorance about how an economy functions, i.e., economic black magic.[1]

10.2 FACTS ABOUT THE GREAT DEPRESSION

10.2.1 Real GDP

The Dow Jones Industrial Average (DJIA) climbed from 161.2 in September 1926 to 362.35 in September 1929, an increase of 124.8 percent. In an attempt to end this apparent speculative bubble, the Federal Reserve increased interest rates early in 1929. We now know that such actions usually lead to a decrease in spending on goods and services, i.e., people borrow less and buy less when interest rates are higher. Thus, the Fed might have unwittingly induced a cyclical downswing that ended up being the Great Depression.

Table 10.1   *US real GDP, 1929–1939*

Year	Billions of 2005 dollars
1929	976.1
1930	892.0
1931	834.2
1932	725.2
1933	715.8
1934	793.7
1935	864.2
1936	977.0
1937	1027.1
1938	991.8
1939	1071.9

Source: FRED: Bureau of Economic Analysis.

Table 10.1 shows that real GDP decreased from $976 billion in 1929 to $716 billion in 1933, a cumulative decrease of 26.7 percent.[2] To put this in perspective, from the end of World War Two through the Great Recession of 2007–2009, the US economy had 12 cyclical downswings. The average decrease in real GDP for these was about 2 percent, and the largest decrease was approximately 4 percent. The 26 percent decrease during the Great Depression was terrible! Even worse, industrial output is thought to have fallen by almost 50 percent.

Output started increasing in the spring of 1933 and grew until May 1937. Table 10.1 indicates that it was above its 1929 value in 1936. It is noteworthy that the Great Depression was essentially over (at least with respect to output) at this time. However, prices increased during this interval.[3] The Fed took steps to fight this inflation via tighter monetary policy, and this temporarily reduced output in the second half of 1937 and in part of 1938. Then it turned up so that by 1939 it was again higher than in 1929.

10.2.2   Unemployment

Table 10.2 implies that the unemployment rate for the civilian labor force in 1929 was a very low 3.15 percent. By early 1933 the unemployment rate for the civilian labor force had increased to 24.8 percent. To put this in perspective, the highest value for unemployment in the 12 recessions from World War Two until the coronavirus pandemic was slightly over 10 percent on two occasions. In addition, between 1929 and 1933 the average number of hours worked per week decreased 26 percent.

Table 10.2   *US labor force and employment, 1929–1940 (annual*
                  averages, in thousands)

Year	Civilian labor force	Employed	Unemployed
1929	49,180	47,630	1,550
1930	49,820	45,480	4,340
1931	50,429	42,400	8,020
1932	51,000	38,940	12,060
1933	51,590	38,760	12,830
1934	52,230	40,890	11,340
1935	52,870	42,260	10,610
1936	53,440	44,410	9,030
1937	54,000	46,300	7,700
1938	54,610	44,220	10,390
1939	55,230	45,750	9,480
1940	55,640	47,520	8,120

Source: *Monthly Labor Review*, July 1948.

The unemployed rate in December 1939 was 17.2 percent, even though output in 1939 was slightly above its 1929 level. Why? The answer has two parts to it. Table 10.2 shows that civilian employment was 47.6 million in 1929, but was only 45.8 million in 1939. More output in 1939 with almost 2 million fewer workers means that labor productivity had increased. The second reason is that the USA had ten years of people growing up and looking for a job. Table 10.2 indicates that the civilian labor force increased from 49.2 million in 1929 to 55.2 million in 1939. The labor supply had increased by 6 million from 1929 to 1939 but there were 2 million fewer jobs.

10.2.3   Prices

The US economy experienced 18 recessions from 1860 until 1929. Prices fell during 16 of the 18 recessions. In 13 of these 16 cases the output turned up rather quickly. This apparently convinced people that the microeconomic conclusion (that every firm can sell all of its output if it cuts prices enough) also held for the entire economy.

From October 1929 until April 1933, the index of general prices for the USA decreased almost 32 percent.[4] But the economy became progressively worse. We know now that deflation can cause a great depression, but at that time it seemed like economic black magic. Apparently, President Roosevelt had no idea why deflation was not working, but he was a realist and, thus, urged firms to stop cutting prices, and workers to stop accepting wage cuts. One highly influential economist at that time, Irving Fisher, wrote a scholarly paper that attempted to explain why deflation can be disastrous, but apparently no one paid any attention to it.[5]

10.2.4   The Stock Market

Most people know that the stock market crashed at the beginning of the Great Depression, but they have no idea how badly it crashed and how long it took to recover. Stocks fell about 11 percent in one day in the third week of October 1929. This would be equivalent to a drop in the Dow of more than 3,000 points recently. The market fell roughly 40 percent during the fall of 1929. It rebounded briefly in 1930 and then continued its downward spiral until July 1932. The DJIA decreased 86.8 percent, from 362.35 in September 1929 to 47.75 in July 1932. Few people know that the market did not return to its 1929 high until approximately October 1954. It took 25 years for the market to recover from its losses in the first three years of the Great Depression!

10.3   SOME CAUSES OF THE GREAT DEPRESSION

The only thing we have to fear is fear itself![6]

If anyone believes that a great depression can never occur again (because we know the appropriate government policies to prevent one) then I suspect that their DNA is similar to those who said that the *Titanic* could never sink. What follows is a list of many events that most economists believe contributed to the Great Depression.[7]

10.3.1   The Stock Market Crash

The decline in stock prices ... and the tremendous decline in real output between 1929 and 1933 are simply seen as part of the same cataclysmic decline of the American economy.[8]

Almost everyone has heard that the stock market crash in the fall of 1929 started the Great Depression. However, usually it is not made clear how this event led to a fall in output and the ensuing total collapse of the economy. One reason that has been suggested is a wealth effect. Lower stock prices mean that people have less wealth, and this induces them to buy less. However, in 1929 only 2 percent of American households held stocks.[9] Thus, any decrease in wealth affected only an extremely small rich portion of the population. They might have consumed less, but this is unlikely to have had a significant effect on aggregate demand and output.

Apparently, the news about the market crash and the newspaper pictures of people committing suicide by jumping out of windows in high buildings created fear about the economy that affected aggregate demand in many ways. First, the demand for consumer durable goods dropped precipitously in the six months immediately after the stock market crashed in 1929. Durable goods production decreased 32.4 percent in 1930.[10] Second, fear caused many businesses to postpone or kill many previously planned investment projects. Investment expenditure decreased a whopping 33.3 percent in 1930. This was followed by decreases of 37 percent and 70 percent, respectively, in 1931 and 1932.[11]

Third, banks are reluctant to make loans when there is widespread fear about the economy. Of course, they must make some loans to obtain the revenue needed to operate, but banks always build up excess reserves when they are afraid that default rates might go up if the economy contracts, i.e., a credit crunch occurs. When people have difficulty borrowing money, they spend less.

All of these actions decreased aggregate demand and, hence, output. Any initial decrease in the output of final goods works its way upstream through the supply chain via Leontief's Law. Also, when firms reduce output they lay off workers. Workers who lose their jobs buy less, and the contraction process is multiplied downstream. In sum, the stock market crash helped to create the Great Depression primarily via the fear that it created for households, firms, and banks, i.e., economic black magic!

10.3.2 Grandma Kovalesky and Financial Disintermediation

Recall that a fundamental principle of macroeconomics is that all saving must be borrowed and spent in order for all GDP to be purchased. When much saving is not borrowed and spent, this financial disintermediation (as it is called) always induces a decrease in output. Three possible reasons for financial disintermediation are: (a) people hoarding money; (b) a credit crunch, i.e., banks are afraid to lend; and (c) bank failures. From 1929 until the end of 1932 thousands of banks shut down.

A story

As mentioned earlier, my Polish grandparents were poorly educated immigrants in the early 1900s. Somehow, they managed to save some money. When the stock market crashed Grandma Kovalesky literally ran to her bank and withdrew all of their funds. Then she had Pappy make a small wooden box. He screwed a hook into the box, put several heavy rocks in, and placed their life savings inside. Then he water-proofed it with hot tar and dropped the box down the out-house hole in the backyard, where it stayed safely for years.

How did this help to create the Great Depression? First, hoarding their savings in the out-house hole meant that these funds could not be borrowed and spent, i.e., financial disintermediation. Secondly, Grandma's run to the bank was what thousands of people did. In many cases, the banks were forced to close because they did not have sufficient funds on hand to satisfy their customers. Banks that are closed do not make loans! Note well, that Grandma's running to the bank and hoarding money in the out-house hole were caused by fear, i.e., black magic again.

10.3.3   Economic Darwinism and the Federal Reserve

As pointed out earlier, Economic Darwinism is undoubtedly a good idea, provided that it is not carried to an extreme. The Federal Reserve has the ability to rescue any bank by lending funds to it quickly. At the time of the Great Depression the Fed would not lend to a bank unless the bank had sufficient collateral. The latter was typically commercial paper, i.e., the IOU papers that firms sign when they borrow from a bank. If a bank did not have sufficient collateral, then the Fed considered them to be inefficient. Thousands of banks fell into this category, and the Fed allowed them to go under. Failed banks do not make loans; ignorance is another cause of economic black magic!

10.3.4   Severe Droughts in the 1930s

[A] massive dust storm 2 miles high traveled 2,000 miles before hitting the east coast on May 11, 1934. … Prairie dirt enshrouded landmarks such as the Statue of Liberty and the US Capitol.[12]

Every spring, farmers borrow heavily to buy seeds, fertilizer, new equipment, etc. They repay their loans after the crops are harvested at the end of the summer. If bad weather significantly reduces agricultural output, then many farm loans will not be repaid. This puts farm banks in jeopardy. The Midwest in the USA experienced record-breaking droughts in the 1930s. Severe droughts undoubtedly made the Great Depression worse. No one knows how many of the thousands of bank failures between 1929 and 1933 were caused by such events.

Although the droughts affected much of the Midwest, the worst conditions were in the south-west, especially in Texas, Oklahoma, New Mexico and Kansas, affecting roughly 100 million acres. Severe dust storms totally destroyed crops and killed livestock. Millions of families abandoned their farms, unable to pay home mortgages as well as annual farm loans. When banks took possession of the farms they had little value, thereby making it more likely that the banks would fail. The severe droughts were a random event that contributed to the perfect storm called the Great Depression.

10.3.5   Deflation

The general consensus is that deflation helped to cause the Great Depression, although there is some controversy about whether a deflation is always bad for an economy. There are several reasons why overall decreases in prices might reduce the demand for a country's output. We shall examine one of these.

A story
Many years ago I was browsing at a local mall and saw a great looking leather jacket at a department store with a price tag of $450. However, it was about one week before Christmas, and I decided to wait until after the holidays when many stores have sales. Sure enough, after New Year's Day the jackets were reduced 50 percent to $225. However, I decided not to buy then, but to wait and see if the price would go even lower. I went back to the store many times per week, and much to my delight, the price kept coming down. Eventually, I bought the fine leather jacket for $75.

The moral of this story is that a decrease in prices might prompt people to buy more, but not if a *deflation psychology* arises. Many consumers will wait until they think that prices have hit rock bottom before they buy. Thus, if each decrease in prices in the early 1930s caused people to expect more reductions, then this might have lowered aggregate demand in the USA. The key is whether a deflation psychology existed, and scholars believe that it did.[13]

10.3.6   The Hawley-Smoot Tariff

In the 1920s the USA pursued isolationist policies, which included the Tariff Act of 1924 that had an average tariff rate of 40 percent. Herbert Hoover promised during his campaign in 1928 that he would increase tariffs on agricultural products, but lobbying by many factions after his election convinced him to broaden the scope of the tariff hikes. The Great Depression was not yet a depression on 17 June 1930 when the Hawley-Smoot Tariff Act was passed. There is disagreement over the average level of tariffs, but a consensus is that it was about 52 percent. The idea was that fewer imports would mean more American jobs, because the country would be buying more domestically produced products. (Does this sound familiar?) From 1929 until 1933 the value of imports of goods and services fell $3.8 billion from $5.9 billion to $2.1 billion.

The decrease in imports meant that the USA's trading partners had fewer exports, and this worsened their depressed economies. The other nations did not send the USA a thank you card. Rather, they levied higher tariffs on US exports, with an estimated average of 60 percent. Consequently, US exports of goods and services fell from $7.0 billion in 1929 to $2.4 billion in 1933, a decrease of $4.6 billion.[14] Thus, the value of US exports decreased much more than US imports. There are no data related to the net effect on jobs, but presumably the USA was a net loser. Higher tariffs in an attempt to increase employment is just plain stupid, i.e., economic black magic.

10.3.7   Higher Tax Rates

As mentioned in Chapter 1, President Herbert Hoover encouraged Congress to increase taxes in 1932. In 1931 a sharp decrease in tax revenue caused the federal budget to go into deficit by $462 million. This prompted Hoover's advisors to argue that confidence in the US government required higher taxes to balance the government's budget. The apparent logic went something like this. 'When a firm loses money, people (perhaps rightly) believe that management does not know what it is doing. Thus, if the government has a budget deficit, this will make people believe that the government is incompetent.'

The Revenue Act of 1932 increased corporate profits taxes by about 14 percent and doubled the estate tax. The maximum personal income tax rate went up from 25 percent to 63 percent. Furthermore, it levied a tax on gasoline (for the first time), and on many other products such as furs, jewelry, stamps, telegraph, telephone, coal, coke, and copper ore. There is a huge consensus that the tax hike was absolutely the worst possible thing to do. People and firms were not spending enough. Higher taxes probably served to decrease aggregate demand, thereby exacerbating a bad situation. It is another example as to how bad economic thinking can lead to actions that make everything fall apart, i.e., black magic.

10.3.8   A Huge Decrease in the Money Supply

When fear prompted people like Grandma and Pappy Kovalesky to hoard their money, then their bank could not lend it. When banks lend less, this typically causes the money supply to go down. In addition to households hoarding money, banks do this also when they are afraid to lend, i.e., when they build up their reserves. Currency in bank vaults is not counted as part of the money supply.

From 1929 through 1933 the value for the money supply went down more than 30 percent. Chapter 2 pointed out that Mitchener and Richardson conclude that the primary cause of this decrease was fear.[15] The ratio of currency to checking account balances increased, and banks built up excess reserves somewhat. Both of these actions were associated with fear, and both served to reduce the money supply. Nobel Laureate Milton Friedman and his colleague

Anna Schwartz have argued persuasively that this monetary contraction was the most important cause of the Great Depression.[16] Furthermore, the Fed could have prevented this, but it did not! Both fear and ignorance = black magic!

When people hoard their savings and when banks are afraid to lend this means that much saving is not borrowed and spent. Consequently, aggregate demand is less than output and this means that some output goes unsold. The latter, in turn, causes firms to reduce output and lay off workers. Laid-off workers spend much less than those who are working, and a downward spiral continues. Also, a large decrease in the money supply always causes prices to fall, i.e., deflation, and we know that deflation psychology can kill an economy.

NOTES

1. Allegedly, many academic economists warned Herbert Hoover about the danger of some of his economic policies, but he accepted the advice of his economic advisors who were highly successful in the business world.
2. All business cycle data here come from National Bureau of Economic Research (2021).
3. Employment was 670 million higher in 1937 than in 1929, but the unemployment rate remained very high primarily because the labor supply had increased by about 4.8 million.
4. The index went from 181 to 124.
5. Fisher (1933).
6. Roosevelt (1933).
7. This is not a complete list, and I doubt if we know all the reasons for the Great Depression.
8. Romer (1990).
9. Galbraith (1990), p. 78.
10. Romer (1990), p. 607.
11. Source: Bureau of Economic Analysis, 'Growth Rates of Key Macro Variables, 1930–39', Washington, DC, Department of Commerce.
12. Klein (2012), p. 1.
13. Hamilton (1992) concludes that the decrease in prices in 1930 was not anticipated, but after that there was a deflation psychology. Contrastingly, Cecchetti (1992) believes that deflation might have been anticipated as early as the end of 1929.
14. These data come from: Bureau of the Census, Historical Statistics of the United States, 1789–1945, Series M 14–41.
15. Mitchener and Richardson (2020).
16. Friedman and Schwartz (1963).

11. The Great Recession: economic black magic II

11.1 INTRODUCTION

Countries that rank high in the Freedom Index tend to also rank high in many measures of economic success. However, too much freedom or not enough freedom can generate economic black magic. Chapter 2 pointed out that scholarly studies have found no consistent relationship between corruption and economic performance. However, many people believe that greed and corruption helped to create the Great Recession of 2007–2009.[1]

I vividly recall a lunch table conversation about economic freedom many years ago. Some very bright professors said that we do not need the government to regulate industries, such as airlines or meat packers. Supposedly, the market will take care of everything. They acknowledged that with no regulation it is likely that some airlines would skimp on maintenance. However, their planes would crash frequently. Eventually, this would scare enough customers away that the bad airline would go bankrupt.

Supposedly, the same applies to meat packers, in an obvious way. My reply was: 'But what about all the people who die from plane crashes or get food poisoning from tainted meat?' Their reply was: 'That is just the collateral damage that is worth it to save the money from no regulation, and to reap the benefits to firms from the freedom that comes with no regulation.'

If the no regulation of airlines and meat packers argument sounds far-fetched, then brace yourself. In 1999 the government dropped a key provision of a law that regulates banks. Critics worried that this would allow banks to make bad loans. Free market proponents argued that the market would regulate banks. Any bank that consistently made bad loans would eventually go under.

Little did these free market advocates realize that too little regulation of banks would help to create the Great Recession, which put the USA and the rest of the world perilously close to Great Depression #2. Furthermore, the fear this created led to anemic economic growth for many years, i.e., negative economic hysteresis existed. The Great Recession of 2007–2009 illustrates the fact that not enough regulation can be a cause of economic black magic.

11.2 THE GLASS-STEAGALL AND GRAMM-LEACH-BLILEY ACTS

On 16 June 1933 Congress passed the Glass-Steagall Act which had many provisions. One was that commercial banks could no longer buy common stock. Before Glass-Steagall, banks could use funds deposited with them to speculate in the booming stock market. When the market crashed, this helped to cause many banks to become insolvent and fail. This provision still exists.

Glass-Steagall had other provisions that are of no concern here.[2] The most important one for our purposes was that commercial banks (hereafter referred to as regular banks or simply banks) could not be affiliated with investment banks. Affiliated means that investment banks could not own a regular bank or vice versa. Also, a holding company could not own both of them. Glass-Steagall did not outlaw banks from doing business with investment banks. Indeed, between 1933 and the late 1990s banks would occasionally use investment banks to find buyers for some of their mortgages. However, Glass-Steagall created a culture that discouraged banks from doing this.

In November 1999, Congress passed the Gramm-Leach-Bliley Act that rescinded the provision of Glass-Steagall that prevented banks from being affiliated with investment banks. It did not take long for such affiliation to occur, and this has been blamed (in part) for the Great Recession. However, such affiliation was minor compared to the change in the culture that it created.[3] It was no longer considered bad for banks to do business with investment banks.

11.3 THE SPECULATIVE BUBBLE IN THE HOUSING MARKET

President Clinton and President George W. Bush encouraged banks to help low-income families obtain home mortgages. The idea was that almost everyone should have a chance to obtain the American dream of owning their own home. Consistent with this, the Fed had a relatively easy monetary policy during most of this time interval. Also, excess foreign saving had been pouring into US banks every year.

Consequently, banks had more than enough funds to lend for buying houses. In fact, they had so many deposits that they relaxed their credit standards in order to lend all of it. High risk mortgage loans called subprime mortgages became commonplace. There is no precise definition for a subprime mortgage, but some scholars have said that this name applies to mortgage loans for those whose credit rating is less than 650. In addition to lowering their credit standards, banks devised innovative types of home mortgages. The most important one was Adjustable Rate Mortgages (ARMs). Roughly 75 percent of subprime mortgages were ARMs.

One incentive for people to borrow and buy a house in the early 2000s was the fact that the average price of a house in the USA had not decreased in any year since World War Two. Also, the Standard and Poor/Case-Shiller Price Index went from 76.9 to 100 from 1990 to 2000, a cumulative increase of 30 percent in ten years.

Then from 2000 until July 2006, the housing price index increased from 100 to 185, a cumulative increase of 85 percent in only six years. These facts suggested that it was possible to gain a tremendous amount of wealth very quickly. For example, if a person had put $10,000 down on a $100,000 house in the year 2000, then this $10,000 would have increased to $95,000 in six years.

All of the above helped to create a speculative bubble in the housing market. Anyone who has used bubble gum knows that as the bubble gets progressively bigger, it becomes more likely that it will burst. Furthermore, the mess on your face will be progressively worse as the size of the bubble increases. The same is true for speculative bubbles and the mess they create in the economy when they explode.

11.4   SUBPRIME DERIVATIVES

There have been many different estimates of the total value of subprime mortgages that existed in 2007; the most conservative estimate being a little more than $1 trillion, and the least conservative being a bit over $3 trillion. How could so much money have been loaned to risky borrowers? In many cases, the people who applied for such loans lied about their incomes and other financial facts when they filled out the application for a home mortgage. Because bank agents often get a commission when they convince people to borrow, many agents presumably looked the other way when they interviewed the potential borrower.

Traditionally, bankers lose their jobs if they approve too many loans that end up in default. This, however, changed when Congress repealed the section of Glass-Steagall. Banks were not concerned that they were lending to people who were likely to default on the loan, because the banks felt free to have investment banks find buyers for their mortgages. The investment banks, in turn, created bond-like assets, called 'subprime derivatives', that were backed by the subprime mortgages. They sold these to investors in the USA and all over the world, including many European banks.

11.5   SUBPRIME DERIVATIVES WERE RATED AS PERFECTLY SAFE

The investment banks told potential buyers that subprime derivatives were perfectly safe, and they earned at least a 1 percent commission on the subprime sales. If a non-trivial percentage of all subprimes were sold by the investment banks then the total commissions would have been in the hundreds of millions of dollars, which will buy a whole lot of tacos. Perhaps this tempted the investment banks to bend the truth when assessing the risk of subprimes. Or maybe they were just stupid when they assessed the risk. However, after the financial crisis of 2007–2009 (that was triggered by defaults on thousands of subprime mortgages) investment banks lowered the credit rating on subprime derivatives to junk status.

Firms who assess the riskiness of assets like stocks and bonds also rated subprime derivatives as very safe. The fees for rating the subprime derivatives were (and still are) paid by the banks and investment banks who were selling them. This created an incentive to exaggerate how safe subprimes were. After the crisis was over, some members of Congress tried to alter this system of payment, but failed.

Investors everywhere (here and abroad) could not resist taking advantage of a low-risk asset that had a good rate of return, i.e., the subprime derivatives. Thus, investment banks had no problem finding buyers for them, and banks had little trouble finding dead beat customers to borrow more than they could afford to repay. Furthermore, many affluent people decided to jump on the gravy train and buy one or more extra houses as investments.

In addition to sales of new subprime derivatives via investment banks, there developed a market where investors who were holding subprimes could sell them if they needed cash. Also, a futures market for subprimes existed, and people were profiting from all of these financial innovations. The gravy train was roaring down the tracks. Everybody was making big money, and apparently everybody was waiting for someone else to blow the whistle on what ended up being a huge scam.

Clearly the credit rating firms and investment banks were dead wrong about how safe the subprime derivatives were. However, when the government questioned them after the Great Recession occurred, they insisted that they had done nothing illegal, because they had not lied. They said that they were just stupid, and it is not illegal to be stupid.

Their argument went something like this. 'Housing prices had been rising about 10 percent per year; housing prices had never decreased since the end of World War Two; thus, it was reasonable to assume that housing prices would continue to increase. Low-income families (and affluent buyers of houses for an investment) would not default on their home mortgages if they were making a lot of money each year as the value of their house appreciated. Thus, subprime mortgages were perfectly safe.'

Allegedly, in 2013, the US Attorney for the Eastern District of California investigated wrongdoing by JP Morgan Chase. A formal complaint, called The Wagner Complaint, was written but never filed. The complaint contained testimony by a former JP Morgan Chase banker, who allegedly warned superiors that risky mortgages were backing subprime derivatives. Eventually, the whistle-blower was fired. In November 2013, JP Morgan Chase made a deal to pay fines of $13 billion to various federal and state agencies, provided that The Wagner Complaint, including the whistle-blower's revelations, did not become public.[4]

From 2009 through 2015, 49 financial institutions paid fines and civil lawsuit settlements whose total was almost $190 billion. However, these funds came from shareholders' money, and did nothing to punish the alleged wrong-doers.[5] Ultimately, only one top banker went to prison for lying about losses to Credit Suisse's mortgage-backed securities portfolio.[6]

11.6   WHY THE SUBPRIME BUBBLE BURST AND CAUSED THE GREAT RECESSION

11.6.1   The Internet Bubble in the 1990s

Speculative bubbles typically grow relatively slowly, and then deflate rapidly when they burst. An example is the internet stock boom of the 1990s. The Nasdaq Composite Index went from 330 in October 1990 to 4,697 in February 2000. Initial public offerings (IPOs) of internet stocks in the early 1990s often sold for $1 per share. By the end of the decade some of these stocks had sky-rocketed up to prices around $100 per share. In some cases, the firms had never made a profit, but their stock price kept rising.

Some people say this was not a speculative bubble. Rather, stock prices increased so much because investors anticipated huge profits in the future. This might have been true to a certain degree, but it is also possible that the unbelievable rise in internet stock prices was a result of the 'greater fool' mentality.[7]

Like all huge speculative bubbles, the internet bubble eventually burst. In the first two years of the twenty-first century many internet firms went bust. The Nasdaq index went down to 1,172 in September 2002, a decrease of about 75 percent from its high in 2000. Some stocks that had been worth close to $100 per share had their price fall to as low as 12.5 cents.

11.6.2   Financial Panic

The housing bubble and bust were the proximate causes of the financial crisis, setting off a vicious cycle of falling house prices and surging foreclosures.[8]

What caused the housing bubble to burst? In addition, how did perhaps only slightly more than $3 trillion of subprime derivatives cause a world financial meltdown when total world financial assets were thought to be $100 trillion to $130 trillion? It seems like the tail was wagging the dog. Furthermore, how did this cause GDP in the USA to fall more than in the previous 11 economic recessions since World War Two? I believe it was economic black magic in the form of fear and panic.

We will get to how fear and panic made everything fall apart, but what caused the fear? Here are some possibilities, relating to the Federal Funds Rate (FFR)[9] and the one-year ARM from 2001 through 2007. The bursting of the internet stock bubble induced the Fed to reduce the FFR from 6 percent to 1 percent in the first few years after the turn of the century. The one-year ARM fell with the FFR, but not as much. The Fed eventually reversed course and increased the FFR from 1 percent in July 2004 to just above 5 percent in July 2006. This was accompanied by an increase in the one-year ARM. Other mortgage rates also increased, but by smaller percentages.

All of this had two negative effects. Higher mortgage rates decreased the demand for new and used houses, thereby creating an excess supply of them. The excess supply caused the price index for houses in the USA to fall slightly (for the first time since World War Two) from 184.3 in April 2006 to 182.6 in August 2006. Also, the increase in the interest rates on ARMs raised monthly mortgage payments for many people who had been struggling to make their payments at lower interest rates.

Apparently, the slight decrease in home prices in 2006 frightened many homeowners, who feared that very soon they might owe more on their home than the home was worth. It is not unreasonable to think that this prompted some of them to decide to default on their loans. The delinquency rate for subprimes financed by ARMs increased from less than 10 percent to roughly 40 percent from 2006 to the end of 2009.[10]

When a speculative bubble exists, smart people keep a sharp eye out for signals that the bubble is about to burst. They want to be the first to get out. The decrease in housing prices and the increase in delinquency rates for subprimes in 2006 represented such signals. The smart money people feared that more mortgage defaults were coming, the housing bubble was about to burst, and the value of subprime derivatives was going to fall tremendously. Somebody somewhere started unloading their holdings of subprime derivatives.

Subprime derivatives were owned by insurance companies, mutual funds, pension funds, conservative banks in the USA who had not issued subprime mortgages, wealthy people both in the USA and abroad, and many European banks. Here is where economic black magic in the form of fear came in.

Recall that subprime derivatives were probably less than 3 percent of all financial assets in the world. Allegedly, only about 1 percent of the subprime derivatives decreased more than 30 percent in value. However, investment banks, brokerage firms, and the banks that had not made bad loans had an inventory of subprime derivatives when the bubble burst, and several were about to go under.

The Fed helped arrange Merrill Lynch to be bought by Bank of America. Wachovia, a top five commercial bank was purchased by Wells Fargo. Also, JP Morgan Chase bought the nation's largest Savings and Loan bank, WAMU. However, the Fed allowed one large investment bank, Lehman Brothers, to go under. This created fear in financial markets that then caused all hell to break loose! Some details are as follows:[11]

- The Reserve Primary Fund (a large money market fund, MMF) had huge holdings of Lehman Brothers paper. Lehman's collapse caused the Reserve Primary Fund to become insolvent.
- This created much fear, which induced investors to pull funds out of all MMFs.
- In order to obtain cash to satisfy their customers, MMFs started selling assets such as 'commercial paper' in such large amounts that the market seized up.
- This, in turn, implied that firms might not be able to raise cash by issuing commercial paper. If so then many firms would not be able to meet payroll deadlines, etc., thereby initiating a significant decrease in commerce, i.e., a crash.
- All of this helped generate fear among stockholders, and led to a prolonged sell-off during which the DJIA went from 19,273 in September 2007 to 10,341 in March 2009, a decrease of almost 50 percent.

11.6.3   From Financial Panic to a Deep Recession

One important consequence of the subprime collapse was a vast change in banks' standards for granting loans. Previously most reasonably safe borrowers had no problem getting a loan. All of a sudden, it seemed as though they could not get any banker's attention. Bank lending standards became tighter than they had been in the previous 25 years.[12] This created a credit crunch, that ultimately reduced aggregate demand and output by approximately 4 percent, well over $500 billion. Firms laid off workers and the unemployment rate exceeded 10 percent. If the Fed and Congress had not responded properly, many people believe that Great Depression #2 would have occurred.

All of this was caused by economic black magic in the form of too much freedom for banks, greed and corruption of those who profited from the subprime scam, fear and panic by those holding subprime derivatives, fear and panic by investors who withdrew billions of dollars from money market funds, and/or dumped their stocks and holdings of subprime derivatives, and the fear that induced banks to withhold loans that were badly needed to keep the economy afloat.

Finally, part of today's thinking is that the economy grew very slowly during the eight years of the Obama Administration. However, Table 4.1 showed that the last three years for Obama were similar in economic performance to the first three years for Trump, before the coronavirus pandemic hit us. Current thinking is roughly correct for the earlier years of the Obama Administration, but he took office in the middle of the Great Recession.

The economy perked up slightly from the end of the Great Recession in June 2009 until roughly the end of 2010. Then for the 12 quarterly periods from the fourth quarter of 2010 through the third quarter of 2013 output creeped up cumulatively by only 4.9 percent, and only 5.5 million jobs were created (almost three million less than in the next three years). As pointed out several times already in this book, this appears to be an example of negative economic hysteresis. The temporary financial crisis of 2007–2009 exerted a negative effect on economic growth for about four years.

NOTES

1. The National Bureau of Economic Research dates the Great Recession as follows: the peak was in December 2007, and the trough was in June 2009.
2. One of these established the Federal Deposit Insurance Corporation (FDIC).
3. See Zandi (2009).
4. Cohen (2015).
5. Cohen (2015).
6. Eisinger (2014).
7. When there is general agreement that an asset is over-valued, speculators will still buy it if they believe that in the near future a 'greater fool' will buy it from them at an even higher price.
8. Blinder and Zandi (2010), p. 2.
9. The FFR is the interest rate that banks charge each other on very short-term loans. This is freely determined by the supply and demand for such loans. However, the Fed indirectly controls this by pumping funds into or out of the banking system when the FFR is about to move outside the Fed's officially stated range for the FFR.
10. Source: Mortgage Bankers Association National Delinquency Survey, 2009.
11. See Zandi (2009), pp. 212–213.
12. Ibid., p. 192.

12. The pandemic: economic black magic III

12.1 INTRODUCTION AND OVERVIEW

As pointed out in Chapter 4, the US economy had been doing OK for about six years when the coronavirus pandemic hit early in 2020. It is significant that the economy's performance was roughly the same during: (a) the last three Obama years with higher corporate tax rates and, allegedly, too many government regulations; and (b) the first three Trump years with (after 2017) lower corporate tax rates, 100 percent write-offs of some investments, and less regulation. It seems as though the years 2014 through 2019 are excellent examples of economic magic!

Then 'all hell broke loose' when the coronavirus pandemic came. The economy collapsed, and there is evidence that most of the collapse was not caused by government ordered shutdowns. As pointed out earlier, one scholarly study suggests that it was caused by well-founded fear.[1] If so, then this is an excellent example of economic black magic. Fear kept people in their homes and drastically reduced spending on many types of goods and services; the negative effects of this spread rapidly throughout almost every sector of the economy.

Fear and government lockdowns significantly reduced or completely devastated the incomes of tens of thousands of restaurants, movie theaters, taverns, cruise ships, airlines, and small businesses of all types. Say's Law meant that the lower incomes for the owners and workers in such businesses reduced their spending, which negatively affected people downstream. Furthermore, Leontief's Law means that workers and firms upstream (who previously supplied the products that were no longer bought) were negatively affected.

At each stage in the transmission process, the reduced incomes and spending of the latest victims generated another round of negative effects upstream and downstream. Some estimates suggest that in the first six months of the pandemic, more than 200,000 businesses shut down. If some of these closed permanently, this represents a decrease in the USA's *useful* capital stock.

Furthermore, the labor force participation rate decreased significantly, in part, because the coronavirus pandemic induced many people to retire early.

Finally, the pandemic helped to create significant bottlenecks in the supply chain. All three events decreased potential output. A severe temporary negative shock (the pandemic before vaccinations) had a lasting negative effect, i.e., negative economic hysteresis existed. The decrease in potential output has acerbated the inflation experienced in recent years.

This chapter proceeds as follows. Section 12.2 reviews the financial panic when the Fed first took drastic steps in response to the pandemic. Sections 12.3 and 12.4 look at the effects of the pandemic on GDP, employment, and unemployment. This is followed in Section 12.5 by an account of the actions of the Fed and the effects of the latter on the US money supply, which increased rapidly during the early years of the pandemic. Finally, section 12.6 reviews data on prices and inflation rates, and the controversy with regard to what caused the inflation rate to increase so rapidly.

12.2   FINANCIAL PANIC AND THE STOCK MARKET

Supposedly, on 26 February 2000, a US health official caused *concern* for COVID-19 to become *panic* by saying that we would probably have to close schools and keep people home, etc.[2] The next day, 27 February 2000, the Dow decreased by 1,200 points, the worst day since 2008. Then the market went from 'bad to worse', by falling tremendously on 9 March and 12 March. Indeed, on Monday morning of 9 March, stocks fell so rapidly that trading was halted for 15 minutes.

On 16 March 2020 the Dow fell 13 percent, the second largest percentage decrease in history, behind only Black Monday in October 1987. What caused this? The Fed surprisingly announced on Sunday, 15 March, at 5 p.m. that it was cutting interest rates to almost zero and buying $700 billion in government bonds. Everyone took this to mean that things were very bad! This generated much fear.

Corporate treasurers and pension fund managers have always considered money market funds, MMFs, almost as good as cash ... and they pay interest.[3] However, the fear created by the Fed's announcement induced a panic, and a run toward cash. We know that fear always induces people to hoard money (recall the story about my Grandma Kovalesky). Thus, on Monday morning of 16 March 2020, corporate treasurers and pension fund managers pulled billions of dollars out of MMFs.

MMFs had to sell bonds to get the cash, but no one wanted to buy them. Everyone was desperate for cash. Investors struggled to unload even safe assets like US Treasury bonds. All of this was bad news for more than the firms who had placed funds in the MMFs. Thousands of companies and communities depend on short-term loans from MMFs to pay their bills on time and to make payroll.[4] All of the above created fear everywhere in financial markets.

This induced a huge decrease in stock prices; the Dow Jones Industrial Index fell 36.8 percent from 14 February 2020 to 23 March 2020. Three terrible days for the stock market were:

1. Black Monday I: 9 March 2020; the Dow decreased 2,014 points.
2. Black Thursday: 12 March 2020; the Dow decreased 2,352 points.
3. Black Monday II: 16 March 2020; the Dow decreased 2,997 points.

Fear also created extreme volatility in the stock market. The CBOE Russell 2000 Volatility Index (a Wall Street fear gauge) hit a record high of 83.2 on 16 March 2020, as compared to its previous record of 82.6 on 19 November 2008 during the Great Recession.[5] In sum, fear induced: (a) panic, (b) extreme financial market volatility, and (c) a run toward cash during both the Great Recession and the pandemic. Indeed, fear might well be the leading cause of economic black magic.[6]

The Dow bounced back rather quickly so that in November 2020 it slightly exceeded its previous high of 14 February 2020. Then it continued to increase rapidly and hit 36,407 in January 2022, an increase of 95.8 percent from its low in March 2020. The price earnings ratio, P/E, has averaged close to 18 over many decades, but at the end of 2021 it was above 30.

Some economists believe that the Fed indirectly caused this run-up via its essentially zero interest rate policy, and rapid increase in the money supply. Their logic is that investors would not accept a zero or negative real interest rate on bonds and bank savings accounts. Thus, they speculated in the stock market and in crypto-currencies, and there was plenty of money available to do this.[7]

12.3   EFFECTS ON OUTPUT

When state and local governments as well as fear shut down a large part of the economy, the effect on GDP from the first to the second quarter of 2020 was extremely large. Table 12.1 shows that real GDP decreased from $19.25 trillion at the end of 2019 to $17.30 trillion six months later, a decline of slightly more than 10 percent in just three months. This was much worse than the previously largest drop in output since World War Two of roughly 4 percent during the Great Recession.

The composition of output changed radically during the pandemic year of 2020. There were essentially no concerts, vacations – especially on cruise ships – sporting events with large crowds, hanging out at taverns, or fine dining. On the other hand, spending was up (in some cases nearly 25 percent) on items such as furniture, home workout equipment, computers, phones, electronic games, and bikes.

Table 12.1   US real GDP from 2019:4 through 2021:4

Period	Quarterly real GDP (annual rates)
2019:4	$19.25 trillion
2020:2	$17.30 trillion
2021:1	$19.06 trillion
2021:4	$19.81 trillion

Source: Federal Reserve Economic Data, US Bureau of Economic Analysis.

The economy gradually improved after it hit bottom and then shot up significantly in early 2021. Table 12.1 shows that real GDP increased from $17.3 trillion in the second quarter of 2020 to $19.06 trillion in the first quarter of 2021, an increase of 10.2 percent. It had returned approximately to its pre-pandemic value in slightly less than one year. Table 12.1 also shows that real GDP continued to increase in 2021, reaching $19.8 trillion in the fourth quarter. Then it turned down minutely in the first quarter of 2022, and again slightly in the second quarter of 2022 (not shown).

Typically, short-term interest rates are lower than long-term rates. However, when the Fed has increased short-term rates in order to fight inflation, this has often caused short-term rates to exceed long-term rates.[8] This situation is referred to as an 'inverted yield curve'. The last six economic downturns were preceded by an inverted yield curve.[9]

An inverted yield curve existed at the end of 2021, and, sure enough, real GDP decreased slightly during the first two quarters of 2022. The de facto definition of a recession is that output goes down for two consecutive quarterly periods. However, economists and politicians disagree as to whether this slight downturn is a recession.

12.4   EFFECTS ON EMPLOYMENT AND UNEMPLOYMENT

Figure 12.1 shows that the US unemployment rate sky-rocketed from 3.5 percent to 14.8 percent immediately after the pandemic hit. This exceeded the previous post-World War Two highs for unemployment in the low 10 percent range in the early 1980s and during the Great Recession. Most of the unemployment involved workers at or near the bottom of the income distribution scale. The bottom 20 percent had employment decrease by 30 percent. Firms with less than 50 workers (primarily retail stores with low paying jobs) laid off more than 25 percent of their workers.

Many people dropped out of the labor force during the pandemic. The Labor Force Participation Rate, LFPR, was 63.4 percent in February 2020. It fell to

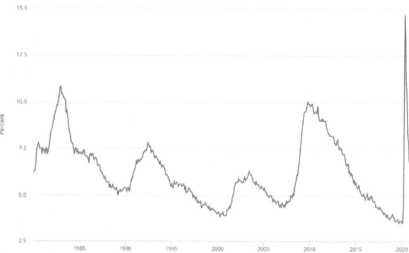

Source: US Bureau of Labor Statistics, Unemployment Rate [UNRATE], retrieved from FRED, Federal Reserve Bank of St. Louis; https://fred.stlouisfed.org/series/UNRATE.

Figure 12.1   US unemployment rate 1980–2020

60.2 percent by April of that year. This amounted to approximately 4.5 million fewer workers. As of August 2021, it had risen slightly to 61.7 percent. By March 2022 the LFPR was up to 62.4 percent, and the labor force had returned to its pre-pandemic value of slightly over 164 million.[10] However, during normal times it would have increased by about 3 million over a two-year period. In brief, during March 2022 the labor supply was roughly 3 million lower than it would have been with no pandemic. Thus, potential output was lower, i.e., negative economic hysteresis was operative.[11]

Many reasons have been given for the decrease in the labor supply. They include: (1) stimulus checks decreased the desire to work for some people; (2) high and extended unemployment benefits kept people at home because their income was higher than if they worked; (3) many workers feared returning to work too quickly because of the virus; (4) the virus closed many childcare facilities and schools, and not all schools fully reopened immediately; thus, many parents had to stay out of the labor force; and (5) at least one million more people than usual retired from February 2020 until the spring of 2021.[12]

From February 2020 through April 2020 total employment in the USA dropped from 158 million to 133.3 million. Then employment increased more or less steadily as GDP went up, and at the end of the first quarter of 2021 total employment was 150.5 million. This was 7.5 million lower than employment when the pandemic began, even though real GDP had returned to its pre-pandemic value.

When output increases faster than employment then labor productivity has increased. However, it is not known if the higher productivity in 2021 reflected previous investments in software and equipment, etc., or simply firms and stores using workers that had been hoarded during the worst of the pandemic. Another contributing factor relates to the facts that: (a) before the virus only 5 percent of all workdays were at home, but allegedly by 2022 roughly 20 percent of all workdays were at home; and (b) labor productivity appears to be slightly higher when people work at home.[13]

12.5   THE FED AND THE MONEY SUPPLY

As pointed out in Section 12.2, the Federal Reserve lowered short-term interest rates to almost zero immediately after the virus struck. In addition, in order to keep long-term interest rates low, the Fed each month bought $80 billion of Treasury bonds, and $40 billion worth of mortgage-backed bonds, i.e., quantitative easing. From March 2020 through the spring of 2021 the Fed bought approximately $1 trillion of mortgage-backed bonds.

Between February 2020 and May 2021, the total value of the Fed's purchases of government bonds exceeded 50 percent of the value for new Treasury bond issues that financed the budget deficits. This implies that the Fed was indirectly monetizing more than half of the government's new debt. The bottom line was that total Fed assets increased tremendously from $5.3 trillion in March 2020 to $8.9 trillion in April 2022, thereby creating an unprecedented rapid increase in the monetary base.

Indeed, the money supply grew at an unbelievably fast rate. The M1 measure of money increased from just under $4 trillion in February 2020 to an astounding $19 trillion in April 2021! A significant portion of this, however, was tied up with a change in the definition of M1. Previously, M1 included coins and currency in circulation, demand deposits, and other checkable accounts. It did not include savings account balances, because these typically limited the amount that could be withdrawn at any one time, thereby making savings accounts less liquid than checking accounts.

However, this restriction on savings accounts was eliminated on 24 April 2020. Consequently, savings account balances are now included in M1. As of May 2020, the new M1 was $16.2 trillion, but slightly more than $11 trillion of this were savings account balances. This implies that the old M1 increased by roughly $1 trillion in only a few months. As always, fear caused a run to cash.

In recent decades, nominal GDP has been more closely related to the M2 measure of money than to the M1 measure.[14] M2 also increased rapidly when the virus hit. It went from $15.4 trillion in February 2020 to $21.5 trillion two years later – an increase of 38.7 percent.[15]

Most economists agree that high and persistent inflation has occurred only when the money supply has grown rapidly and continuously. However, an incredibly high monetary growth rate for a brief interval does not necessarily ensure persistently high inflation rates. If increases in the money supply are hoarded out of fear, then the inflationary consequences can initially be minimal. This is exactly what happened in 2020, because the velocity of M2 decreased sharply by more than 20 percent in that year.[16]

The danger is that the hoarded money will eventually be spent, and this appears to be what has happened. If the recently high inflation rate leads eventually to large wage rate increases (to catch up, so to speak) then this can create a 'wage–price spiral' which is difficult to reverse and, hence, might last for years. This would represent another example of negative economic hysteresis.

12.6   PRICES

We now [30 June 2022] understand better how little we understand about inflation.[17]

Prices went down minutely when the virus attacked. Figure 12.2 shows that the CPI for all urban consumers was 259.0 in February of 2020 and fell slightly to 255.9 by May of that year. Over the next 12 months the CPI increased 4.96 percent to 268.6. We know that the CPI still has a slight upward bias. As pointed out in an earlier chapter, the Fed's preferred measure of prices and inflation is the Personal Consumption Expenditure (PCE) deflator. From May 2020 through May 2021 the PCE deflator increased 3.9 percent.

The yearly inflation rate as of the spring of 2021 was far from even across the board. Some prices shot up tremendously. For example, the prices of used cars increased almost 20 percent from the winter through the spring of 2021. This alone pushed the CPI up by 0.5 percent. Airline fares were up more than 24 percent, and gasoline price increased about 60 percent. By the spring of 2022 gasoline prices had roughly doubled from their pre-pandemic value.

The Standard and Poor, Case-Shiller national home price index had reached an all-time high of roughly 160 before the Great Recession. But by 2012 it had fallen to about 120, only to rise steadily after that. In spite of the pandemic, the housing price index increased by more than 11 percent from March 2020 until March 2021. Then housing prices shot up almost 20 percent from 239.3 in February 2021 to 286.7 in February 2022.[18]

From May of 2021 until April 2022 the CPI increased 7.4 percent. As might be expected, there is controversy with respect to the underlying cause of this relatively high inflation rate. The Republicans claim that it is caused by the huge increase in the money supply, as well as the generous stimulus checks

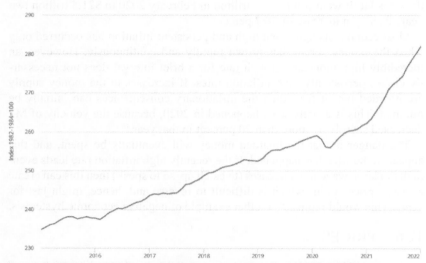

Source: US Bureau of Labor Statistics, Consumer Price Index for All Urban Consumers: All
Items in US City Average [CPIAUCSL], retrieved from FRED, Federal Reserve Bank of St.
Louis; https://fred.stlouisfed.org/series/CPIAUCSL.

Figure 12.2   Consumer price index for all urban consumers 2015–2022

initiated by the Biden Administration. On the other hand, Democrats maintain
that the root cause of this high inflation lies on the supply side, i.e., supply
chain bottlenecks and the decrease in potential output as described above.

In 1890 the English economist Alfred Marshall published a textbook that
dominated the field for many decades. Apparently, it was the first book to
officially declare that prices were determined by the interaction of supply
and demand. (I have always wondered why it took the human race so long to
figure this out.) Allegedly, he once said that it is nonsense to debate whether
prices are determined either by supply or demand. This, he maintained, was
equivalent to arguing over which blade in a pair of scissors does the cutting.

It might be impossible to determine the extent to which the high inflation
rate of 2021–2022 was caused by increased demand or decreased supply.
However, one thing is certain. Output went down in the first half of 2022 even
though prices increased rapidly. It is impossible for prices to rise and output
to fall unless aggregate supply has decreased – the position of the Democratic
party.

Moreover, there is evidence that households have been on a spending
spree via the use of funds they had accumulated from the stimulus checks
and the extra saving out of earned income during the worst of the pandemic.

Consequently, at least part of the inflation was caused by an increase in aggregate demand, i.e., the Republican position. The Republicans and the Democrats are both partially correct.

NOTES

1. Goolsbee and Syverson (2020).
2. Leonard (2022), p. 262.
3. A MMF is a mutual fund that invests in very short-term interest earning assets. Some of these are 30-, 60-, and 90-day government bonds, called Treasury Bills, and very short-term IOUs of corporations, called commercial paper.
4. Such loans are needed because inflows of cash often do not match the need for huge outflows to meet payrolls, pay suppliers, etc.
5. Source: FRED, 'CBOE Russell 5000 Volatility Index', Chicago Board Options Exchange.
6. Cajner et al. (2020).
7. For example, see the excellent book by Leonard (2022).
8. Historically, economists have compared the nominal interest rate on ten-year Treasury bonds with the rate on two-year Treasury bonds. However, Engstrom and Sharpe (2018) claim that the difference between the yields on 3-month versus 18-month Treasury bills predicts better. It is noteworthy that the newer measure did not predict the slight decrease in output that took place in the first two quarters of 2022.
9. An inverted yield curve in the 1960s predicted a cyclical downswing that did not occur.
10. Source: FRED, 'Labor Force Participation Rate', US Bureau of Labor Statistics.
11. This does not mean that potential output will always be lower. It implies that perhaps in future years potential output will be less than it would have been without the negative economic hysteresis.
12. See a highly readable account of this in Tanzi and Sasso (2021).
13. Harrison (2022).
14. M2 includes everything in M1 plus MMF deposits and small time deposits.
15. Source: FRED, M2, Board of Governors of the Federal Reserve System.
16. The velocity of money is defined as [the nominal value of GDP] divided by [the nominal money supply]. It is, in essence, how often each year a typical dollar is spent to buy goods or services. The velocity of M2 went from 1.38 to 1.10 during 2020.
17. Powell (2022).
18. Source: FRED, 'S&P/Case-Shiller US National Home Price Index', Dow Jones Indices LLC.

Bibliography

Acemoglu, Daron, and Pascual Restrepo (2017a), 'Robots and jobs: evidence from US labor markets', NBER Working Paper No. 23285, Cambridge, MA: National Bureau of Economic Research, March.

Acemoglu, Daron, and Pascual Restrepo (2017b), 'Robots and jobs: evidence from the US', *Vox*, CEPR Policy Portal, 10 April.

Acemoglu, Daron, and James Robinson (2012), *Why Nations Fail*, New York: Crown Business.

Ahmad, Eatzaz, Muhammad Aman Ullah and Muhammad Irfanullah Arfeen (2012), 'Does corruption affect economic growth?', *Latin American Journal of Economics*, 49(2), 277–305.

Akerlof, George A. (2002), 'Behavioral macroeconomics and macroeconomic behavior', *American Economic Review*, 92(3), 411–433.

Alesina, Alberto, and Dani Rodrik (1994), 'Distributive politics and economic growth', *Quarterly Journal of Economics*, 109(2), 465–490.

Allen, Edward (2016), 'How to help workers laid low by trade … and why we haven't', *PSA News Hour*, 16 November, p. 3.

Andersen, Lill, and Ronald Babula (2009), 'The link between openness and long-run economic growth', *Journal of International Commerce and Economics*, 2, 31–50.

Andrews, Isaiah, and Maximilian Kasy (2017), 'Identification of and correction for publication bias', NBER Working Paper No. 23298, Cambridge, MA: National Bureau of Economic Research, March.

Atkinson, Tony, Thomas Piketty and Emmanuel Saez (2011), 'Top incomes in the long run of history', *Journal of Economic Literature*, 49(1), 3–71.

Auten, Gerald, and David Splinter (2019), 'Top 1% income shares: comparing estimates using tax data', *American Economic Association Papers and Proceedings*, 109, 307–311.

Autor, David, and David Dorn (2013), 'The growth of low-skill service jobs and the polarization of the US labor market', *American Economic Review*, 103(5), 1553–1597.

Autor, David, David Dorn and Gordon H. Hanson (2013), 'The China syndrome: local labor market effects of import competition in the US', *American Economic Review*, 103(6), 2121–2168.

Autor, David, David Dorn, Gordon H. Hanson, Gary Pisano and Pian Shu (2016), 'Foreign competition and domestic innovation: evidence from US patents', NBER Working Paper No. 22879, Cambridge, MA: National Bureau of Economic Research, December.

Balvers, Ronald J., and Norman C. Miller (1992), 'Factor demand under conditions of product demand and supply uncertainty', *Economic Inquiry*, 30(3), 544–555.

Banerjee, Abhijit V., and Esther Duflo (2003), 'Inequality and growth: what can the data say?', *Journal of Economic Growth*, 8(3), 267–299.

Barro, Robert J. (2000), 'Inequality and growth in a panel of countries', *Journal of Economic Growth*, 5, 5–32.

Bartel, A., C. Ichniowski and K. Shaw (2007), 'How does information technology really affect productivity? Plant level comparisons of product innovation, process improvement, and worker skills', *Quarterly Journal of Economics*, **122**(4), 1721–1758.

Baughman, Laura M., and Joseph F. Francois (2019), 'Trade and American jobs: the impact of trade on US and state level employment: 2019 update', *Trade Partnership Worldwide for Business Roundtable*, February.

Bell, Brian, and Stephen Machin (2018), 'Minimum wages and firm value', *Journal of Labor Economics*, **36**(1), 159–195.

Benedict, Carl, and Michael A. Osborne (2013), 'The future of employment: how susceptible are jobs to computerization?', Working Paper, Oxford: Oxford University.

Bergsten, Fred, as quoted in Edward Allen (2016), 'How to help workers laid low by trade … and why we haven't', *PSA News Hour*, 16 November, p. 3.

Blackburn, K., N. Bose and M. E. Haque (2006), 'The incidence and persistence of corruption in economic development', *Journal of Economic Dynamics and Control*, **30**(12), 2447–2467.

Blanchard, O. J., and L. H Summers (1988), 'Hysteresis and the European unemployment problem', in *Unemployment, Hysteresis and the Natural Rate Hypothesis*, ed. R. Cross, Oxford: Basil Blackwell, 306–364.

Blinder, Alan S., and Mark Zandi (2010), 'How the great recession was brought to an end', https://www.princeton.edu/~blinder/End-of-Great-Recession.pdf.

Bloom, Nicholas, Mirko Draca and John van Reenen (2016), 'Trade induced technical change? The impact of Chinese imports on innovation, IT, and productivity', *Review of Economic Studies*, **83**(1), 87–117.

Brynjolfsson, Eryk, A. Collis, W. E. Diewart, F. Eggers and K. J. Fox (2019), 'GDP-B: accounting for the value of new and free goods in the digital economy', NBER Working Paper No. 25695, Cambridge, MA: National Bureau of Economic Research, March.

Buchholz, Todd G. (1989), *New Ideas from Dead Economists*, New York: New American Library, Penguin Books.

Budiman, Abby (2020), 'Key findings about US immigrants', Pew Research Center, August.

Bugamelli, M., F. Schivardi and R. Zizza (2008), 'The Euro and firm restructuring', NBER Working Paper No. 14454, Cambridge, MA: National Bureau of Economic Research, October.

Bureau of the Census, 'Historical Statistics of the United States, 1789–1945', Series M 14–41, Washington, DC.

Bureau of Economic Analysis, 'Growth Rates of Key Macro Variables, 1930–39', Washington DC: Department of Commerce.

Byrne, David, and Carol Corrado (2020), 'Accounting for innovation in consumer digital services: IT still matters', NBER Working Paper No. 26010, Cambridge, MA: National Bureau of Economic Research, February.

Caer, A. P. (1996), 'Technology, employment, and the distribution of income: Leontief at 90', *Economic Systems Research*, **8**(4), 315–340.

Cajner, Tomax, Leland D. Crane, Ryan A. Decker, John Griggsby, Adrian Hamins-Puertolas, Erik Hurst, Christopher Kurz and Ahu Yildrimax (2020), 'The US labor market during the beginning of the pandemic recession', NBER Working Paper No. 27159, Cambridge, MA: National Bureau of Economic Research, May.

Caliendo, Lorenzo, Maximiliano Dvorkin and Fernando Parro (2015), 'The impact of trade on labor market dynamics', NBER Working Paper No. 21149, Cambridge, MA: National Bureau of Economic Research, May.

Card, David, and Alan B. Krueger (1995), 'Time-series minimum-wage studies: a meta-analysis', *American Economic Review*, **85**(2), 238–243.

Case, Karl, Robert Shiller and Anne Thompson (2012), 'What have they been thinking? Home buyer behavior in hot and cold markets', NBER Working Paper No. 18400, Cambridge, MA: National Bureau of Economic Research, September.

Cass, Oren (2018), *The Once and Future Worker*, New York: Encounter Books.

Cecchetti, Stephen G. (1992), 'Prices during the great depression: was the deflation of 1930–1932 really unanticipated?', *American Economic Review*, **82**(1), 141–156.

Chatterjee, Satuajit (2005), 'Ores and scores: two cases of how competition led to productivity miracles', *Business Review*, Philadelphia, PA: Federal Reserve Bank of Philadelphia.

Clemens, Jeffery (2021), 'How do firms respond to minimum wage increases', *Journal of Economic Perspectives*, **35**(1), 51–72.

Cohen, William D. (2015), 'How Wall Street's bankers stayed out of jail', *The Atlantic*, September.

Congressional Budget Office (2019), *The Effects on Employment and Family Income of Increasing the Federal Minimum Wage*, Washington, DC: Congress of the United States, Congressional Budget Office.

Conniff, Richard (2011), 'What the Luddites really fought against', *Smithsonian Magazine*, March.

Craighead, William, and Norman C. Miller (2010), 'The causes of and gains from intertemporal trade', *Journal of Economic Education*, **41**(3), 275–291.

Crook, Clive (2006), 'The height of inequality', *The Atlantic*, September.

Cross, Rod (1993), 'On the foundations of hysteresis in economic systems', *Economics and Philosophy*, **9**(1), 53–74.

Dixit, Avinash (1992), 'Investment and hysteresis', *Journal of Economic Perspectives*, **6**(1), 107–132.

Dollar, D., and A. Kray (2003), 'Institutions, trade, and growth', *Journal of Monetary Economics*, **50**(1), 133–162.

Draca, Mirko, Stephen Machin and John Van Reenen (2011), 'Minimum wages and firm profitability', *American Economic Journal: Applied Economics*, **3**(1), 129–151.

Eadicicco, Lisa (2014), 'Uber creating jobs', *Business Insider*, 6 June.

Edwards, S. (1998), 'Openness, productivity, and growth: what do we really know?', *Economic Journal*, **108**(447), 383–398.

Eisinger, Jesse (2014), 'Why only one top banker went to jail for the financial crisis', *New York Times Magazine*, 30 April.

Engstrom, Eric, and Steve Sharpe (2018), 'The near-term forward yield spread as a leading indicator: a less distorted mirror', *Finance and Economics Discussion Series 2018-055*, Washington, DC: Board of Governors of the Federal Reserve System.

Faccio, Mara, and Luigi Zingales (2017), 'Political determinants of competition in the mobile telecommunication industry', NBER Working Paper No. 23041, Cambridge, MA: National Bureau of Economic Research, January.

Fadicicco, Lisa (2014), 'Uber says it's creating 20,000 jobs per month', *Business Insider*, 6 June.

Feenstra, R. C., and D. E. Weinstein (2017), 'Globalization, markups and US welfare', *Journal of Political Economy*, **125**(4), 1040–1074.

Fichte, Jonathan Gottlieb (1800), *The Vocation of Man*, quoted in 'The Butterfly Effect: everything you need to know about this powerful mental model' (2017), *Farnam Street* blog, https://www.fs.blog/2017/08/the-butterfly-effect/.

Fisher, Irving (1933), 'The debt–deflation theory of great depressions', *Econometrica*, **1**(4), 337–357.

Forbes, Kristin J. (2000), 'A reassessment of the relationship between inequality and growth', *American Economic Review*, **90**(4), 869–887.

Foster, Lucia, John Haltiwanger and C. J. Krizan (2001), 'Aggregate productivity growth: lessons from microeconomic evidence', in *New Developments in Productivity Analysis*, ed. Charles R. Hulten, Edwin R. Dean and Michael J. Harper, Chicago: University of Chicago Press, 303–372.

Frankel, Jeffrey, and David Romer (1999), 'Does trade cause growth?', *American Economic Review*, **89**(3), 379–399.

Freeman, R., and M. Kleiner (2005), 'The last American shoe manufacturers', *Industrial Relations*, **44**(2), 307–330.

Frey, Carl Benedikt, and Michael A. Osborne (2013), 'The future of employment: how susceptible are jobs to computerization?', Working Paper, Oxford: Oxford University, 17 September.

Friedman, Milton (1962), *Capitalism and Freedom*, Chicago: University of Chicago Press.

Friedman, Milton, and Anna Schwartz (1963), *A Monetary History of the United States, 1867–1960*, Princeton, NJ: Princeton University Press.

Galbraith, John Kenneth (1990), *The Great Crash, 1929*, Boston, MA: Houghton Mifflin.

Geloso, Vincent J. (2019), 'The reality of income inequality', *Fraser Forum*, 9 January.

Geloso, Vincent J., Phillip Magness, John Moore and Phillip Schlosser (2018), 'How pronounced is the U-curve? Revisiting income inequality in the United States, 1917–1945', Working Paper, https://ssrn.com/abstract=2985234.

Ghiselli, Luca (2018), 'The 4th industrial revolution and patent data', *Market Mogul*, February.

Golub, Stephen (1995), *Comparative and Absolute Advantage in the Asia-Pacific Region*, San Francisco, CA: Federal Reserve Bank of San Francisco.

Goolsbee, Austan, and Chad Syverson (2020), 'Fear, lockdown, and diversion: comparing drivers of pandemic economics decline', NBER Working Paper No. 27432, Cambridge, MA: National Bureau of Economic Research, June.

Gordon, Robert J. (2012), 'Is US economic growth over? Faltering innovation confronts the six headwinds', NBER Working Paper No. 18315, Cambridge, MA: National Bureau of Economic Research, August.

Gramm, Phil, and John Early (2019a), 'The myth of wage stagnation', *Wall Street Journal*, 18–19 May, p. A15.

Gramm, Phil, and John Early (2019b), 'The myth of American inequality', *Wall Street Journal*, 10 August, p. A14.

Griswold, Daniel (2011), *The Trade-Balance Creed: Debunking the Belief that Imports and Trade Deficits are a Drag on Growth*, Washington, DC: Center for Trade Policy Studies, Cato Institute.

Hamilton, James D. (1992), 'Was the deflation during the great depression anticipated?', *American Economic Review*, **82**(1), 157–178.

Harrison, David (2022), 'Economy gets tech-spending boost', *Wall Street Journal*, 28 March, p. A2.

Hirsch, Barry (2008), 'Sluggish institutions in a dynamic world: can unions and industrial competition coexist?', *Journal of Economic Perspectives*, **22**(1), 153–176.

Hochberg, Fred P. (2020), *Trade is Not a Four Letter Word*, New York: Avid Reader Press.

Hrdy, Camilla A. (2017), 'Technological un/employment', Working Paper, Kent, OH: Kent State University. https://www.law.nyu.edu/sites/default/files/upload _documents/Camilla%20Hrdy_0.pdf.

Jones, Ronald W., and Jose Scheinkman (1977), 'The relevance of the two-sector production model in trade theory', *Journal of Political Economy*, **85**(5), 909–935.

Kambayashi, Satoshi (2014), 'The onrushing wave – the future of jobs', *The Economist*, January.

Kato, A., and T. Sato (2015), 'Greasing the wheels? The effect of corruption in regulating manufacturing sectors of India', *Canadian Journal of Development Studies*, **36**(4), 459–483.

Keynes, John M. (1932), 'Economic possibilities for our grandchildren (1930)', in *Essays in Persuasion*, New York: Harcourt Brace.

Keynes, John M. (1936), *General Theory of Employment, Interest, and Money*, New York: Harcourt Brace.

Klein, Christopher (2012), '10 things you may not know about the dust bowl', *History Stories*, August, updated March 2019.

Kosten, Dan (2018), 'Immigrants as economic contributors: complementing not competing', https://immigrationforum.org/article/immigrants-economic-contributors -complementing-not-competing/.

Kremer, Michael (1993), 'The O-Ring theory of economic development', *Quarterly Journal of Economics*, **108**(3), 551–575.

Leonard, Christopher (2022), *The Lords of Easy Money: How the Federal Reserve Broke the American Economy*, New York: Simon & Schuster.

Leung, Justin (2021), 'Minimum wage and real wage inequality: evidence from pass-through to retail sales', *Review of Economics and Statistics*, **103**(4), 754–769.

Li, Hongyi, and Heng-fu Zou (1998), 'Income inequality is not harmful for growth: theory and evidence', *Review of Development Economics*, **2**(3), 318–334.

Marx, Karl (1867), *Das Kapital*, Hamburg: Verlag von Meisner Publishing.

Matthews, Dylan (2018), 'A new study says much of the rise in inequality is an illusion. Should you believe it?', *Vox*, January.

Mauro, P. (1995), 'Corruption and economic growth', *Quarterly Journal of Economics*, **110**(3), 681–712.

Melitz, Marc J. (2003), 'The impact of trade on intra-industry reallocations and aggregate productivity growth', *Econometrica*, **71**(6), 1695–1725.

Melitz, Marc J., and Stephen J. Redding (2013), 'Firm heterogeneity and aggregate welfare', NBER Working Paper No. 18113, Cambridge, MA: National Bureau of Economic Research, March.

Melitz, Marc J., and Stephen J. Redding (2014), 'Missing gains from trade?', NBER Working Paper No. 19810, Cambridge, MA: National Bureau of Economic Research.

Melitz, Marc J., and Stephen J. Redding (2021), 'Trade and innovation', NBER Working Paper No. 28945, Cambridge, MA: National Bureau of Economic Research, June.

Meon, P., and L. Weill (2010), 'Is corruption an efficient grease?', *World Development*, **38**(10), 244–259.

Meyer, Bruce D., and James X. Sullivan (2008), 'Changes in the consumption, income, and well-being of single mother headed families', *American Economic Review*, **98**(5), 2221–2241.

Meyer, Bruce D., and James X. Sullivan (2009), 'Five decades of consumption and income poverty in the US', NBER Working Paper No. 14827, Cambridge, MA: National Bureau of Economic Research, March.

Meyer, Bruce D., and James X. Sullivan (2011), 'Viewpoint: further results on meas-uring the well-being of the poor using income and consumption', *Canadian Journal of Economics*, **44**(1), 52–87.

Meyer, Bruce D., and James X. Sullivan (2012), 'Identifying the disadvantaged: official poverty, consumption poverty, and the new supplemental poverty measure', *Journal of Economic Perspectives*, **26**(3), 111–131.

Miller, Norman C. (1968), 'A general equilibrium theory of international capital flows', *Economic Journal*, **78**(310), 312–320.

Mishel, Lawrence, Elise Gould and Josh Bivens (2015), 'Wage stagnation in nine charts', Economic Policy Institute, January.

Mitchener, Kris James and Gary Richardson (2020), 'Contagion of fear', NBER Working Paper No. 26859, Cambridge, MA: National Bureau of Economic Research, March.

Mo, Pak Hung (2001), 'Corruption and economic growth', *Journal of Comparative Economics*, **29**(1), 66–79.

Moosa, Imad A. (2021), *Controversies in Economics and Finance: Puzzles and Myths*, Cheltenham, UK and Northampton, MA, USA: Edward Elgar Publishing.

Mortgage Bankers Association National Delinquency Survey (2009).

Nam, Pham D. (2012), 'Report: the economic benefits of commercial GPS use in the US, and the costs of potential disruption', NDP Consulting, https://www.gps/gov .advisory.meetings.

National Bureau of Economic Research (2021), *US Business Cycle Expansions and Contractions*, Cambridge MA.

OECD (2022), Income inequality (indicator). https://data.oecd.org/inequality/income -inequality.htm.

Pavcnik, Nina (2002), 'Trade liberalization, exit, and productivity improvements: evi-dence from Chilean plants', *Review of Economic Studies*, **69**(1), 117–146.

Payne, Keith (2017), *The Broken Ladder: How Inequality Affects the Way We Think, Live, and Die*, New York: Penguin Books.

Pen, Jan (1971), *Income Distribution*, Harmondsworth: Penguin.

Persson, T., and G. Tabellini (1991), 'Is inequality harmful for growth: theory and evidence', NBER Working Paper No. 3599, Cambridge, MA: National Bureau of Economic Research, January.

Philippon, Thomas (2019), *The Great Reversal: How America Gave Up on Free Markets*, Cambridge, MA: Belknap Press of Harvard University Press.

Piketty, Thomas, and Emmanuel Saez (2003), 'Income inequality in the United States, 1913–1998', *Quarterly Journal of Economics*, **118**(1), 1–39.

Piketty, Thomas, Emmanuel Saez and Gabriel Zucman (2018), 'Distributional national accounts: methods and estimates for the United States', *Quarterly Journal of Economics*, **133**(2), 553–609.

Powell, Jerome (2022), as quoted by Nick Timiras and Tom Fairless, 'Powell fears inflation more than a recession', *Wall Street Journal*, 30 June, p. A2.

Renkin, T., C. Montialoux and M. Siegenthaler (2022), 'The pass-through of minimum wages into US retail prices: evidence from supermarket scanner data', *Review of Economics and Statistics*, **104**(5), 890–908.

Ricardo, David, (1817), *The Principles of Political Economy and Taxation*, Mineola, NY: Dover Publications.

Richards, Julian, and Elizabeth Schaefer (2016), *Jobs Attributable to Foreign Direct Investment in the United States*, Washington, DC: Office of Trade and Economic Analysis, US Department of Commerce.

Rifkin, Jeremy (1995), *The End of Work: The Decline of the Global Labor Force and the Dawn of the Post Market Era*, New York: G. P. Putnam.

Riquier, Andrea (2017), '800,000 factory jobs were lost to Chinese imports, but the US is better off, researchers say', *Capitol Report*, 16 May.

Romer, Christina (1990), 'The great crash and the onset of the great depression', *Quarterly Journal of Economics*, **103**(3), 597–624.

Romer, Paul (1994), 'The origins of endogenous growth', *Journal of Economic Perspectives*, **8**(1), 3–22.

Roosevelt, Franklin D. (1933), Inaugural Address. https://avalon.law.yale.edu/20th_century/froos1.asp.

Rosen, Sherwin (1981), 'The economics of superstars', *American Economic Review*, **71**(5), 845–858.

Ross, Alec (2015), *The Industries of the Future*, New York: Simon & Schuster.

Rotman, David (2013), 'How technology is destroying jobs', *MIT Review*, June.

Samuelson, Paul A. (1939), 'Interactions between the multiplier analysis and the principle of acceleration', *Review of Economic Statistics*, **21**(2), 75–78.

Sawhill, Isabel (2018), *The Forgotten Americans: An Economic Agenda for a Divided Nation*, New Haven, CT: Yale University Press.

Say, John Baptiste (1803), *A Treatise on Political Economy*, New York: Augustus M. Kelley, 1971.

Schumpeter, Joseph (1942), *Capitalism, Socialism, and Democracy*, New York: Harper and Brothers.

Scott, Robert E., and Zane Mokhiber (2020), 'Growing China trade deficit cost 3.7 million American jobs between 2001 and 2018', Washington, DC: Economic Policy Institute, January.

Seib, Gerald F. (2020), 'In coronavirus fight, uncertainty emerges as the new enemy', *Wall Street Journal*, 25 May.

Semuels, Alana (2018), 'How the "losers" in America's trade policies got left behind', *The Atlantic*, 19 October.

Sharpin, A. D., and R. H. Mabry (1986), 'Does more technology create unemployment?', Washington DC: Cato Institute Policy Analysis No. 68, 18 March.

Shefrin, Hersh (2020), 'Great depression economics 101: what historical numbers and charts from the great depression foretell about the economy and stock market', *Post*, 12 April.

Simon, Ruth (2020), 'Chain reaction', *Wall Street Journal*, 21–22 March, p. B1.

Smirnov, Sergey (2015), 'Economic fluctuations in Russia (from the later 1920s to 2015)', *Russian Journal of Economics*, **1**(2), 130–153.

Smith, Adam (1776), *An Inquiry into the Nature and Causes of the Wealth of Nations*, London: W. Strahan and T. Cadell; reprinted version, ed. Edwin Cannan, New York: The Modern Library, Random House, 1937.

Solow, Robert (1956), 'A contribution to the theory of economic growth', *Quarterly Journal of Economics*, **70**(1), 65–94.

Sowell, Thomas (2019), *Discrimination and Disparities*, New York: Basic Books.

Stolper, Wolfgang F., and Paul Samuelson (1941), 'Protection and real wages', *Review of Economic Studies*, **9**(1), 58–73.

Tanzi, Alexandre, and Michael Sasso (2021), 'Covid early retirees top 3 million in US, Fed Research Shows', *Bloomberg*, US Edition, Markets.

Tegmark, Max (2017), *Life 3.0: Being Human in the Age of Artificial Intelligence*, New York: Vintage Books.

Temin, Peter (2010), 'The great recession and the great depression', *Daedalus*, **139**(4), 115–124.

Thaler, Richard H. (2016), 'Behavioral economics: past, present, and future', *American Economic Review*, **106**(7), 1577–1600.

Tirole, Jean (2017), *Economics for the Common Good*, Princeton, NJ: Princeton University Press.

Toffler, Alvin (1970), *Future Shock*, New York: Random House.

US Department of Labor (2020), *Trade Adjustment Assistance for Workers Program: FY Annual Report*, Washington, DC.

Veld, Jan in 't (2019), 'The economic benefits of the EU single market in goods and services', *Journal of Policy Modeling*, **41**(5), 803–818.

Warnock, Francis E., and Veronica Cacdac Warnock (2006), 'International capital flows and US interest rates', NBER Working Paper No. 12560, Cambridge, MA: National Bureau of Economic Research, October.

Weintraub, Pamela (2010), 'The doctor who drank infectious broth, gave himself an ulcer, and solved a medical mystery', *Discover*, April.

West, Darrell M. (2018), *The Future of Work: Robots, AI, and Automation*, Washington, DC: Brookings Institution Press.

Wilkinson, R., and K. Pickett (2010), *The Spirit Level: Why Greater Equality Makes Societies Stronger*, New York: Bloomsbury.

Winick, Erin (2018), 'Every study we could find on what automation will do to jobs, in one chart', *MIT Technology Review*, January.

Yang, Andrew (2018), *The War on Normal People*, New York: Hachette Books.

Zandi, Mark (2009), *Financial Shock*, Upper Saddle River, NJ: FT Press, Pearson Education.

Index

Printed and bound by CPI Group (UK) Ltd, Croydon, CR0 4YY

16/04/2025

14658434-0003